12/8/99 FAIR NOT PLANNED
ACROSS STREET
FROM LUNCH.
??

# THE ATLANTIS CONNECTION

## BEYOND THE MYTH AND LEGEND TO THE HERE AND NOW!



W.T. SAMSEL

ISBN 0-9666607-0-6
Published by
Starfire Publishing
Sedona, Arizona

Cover design by
Tiagorrah of Poseidon

Printed by
Mission Possible Commercial Printing
P.O. Box 1495, Sedona, AZ 86339

## To the Truth Seekers:

*I would put forth the proposition that spiritual wisdom is ancient truth and that the present civilization lives in ignorance and illusion. I will now impart unto the reader a great volume of knowledge through my interpreter, thus I shall attempt to do so simply and in a concise manner so that there will be understanding.*

*To the one who now holds these printed words in hand, greetings and blessings. I expect that which is contained herein to awaken the consciousness and to stimulate thought. I would that it promote spiritual progression and enlightenment and aid in the transition to a new level of consciousness and perception at this pivotal time in the history of the Earth and mankind.*

— Tiagorrah

Information imparted by Tiagorrah of Poseidon is presented in italics throughout. — W.T. Samsel

# THE ATLANTIS CONNECTION

## CONTENTS

## CONTENTS

# INTRODUCTION

Solon of Athens was a Greek philosopher and statesman who would later come to be regarded as the "wisest of the seven sages." These were seven politicians who carried the Greek civilization through the critical sixth century B.C. In the year 594 B.C., Solon revised Athenian law and government. He presented an alternative to forced rule. Today we regard ancient Athens as the cradle of democracy.

In 590 B.C., Solon visited the land of Egypt. He traveled through the port of Naucratis, and then on to the city of Sais in the Nile delta. There he made several visits to the great temple of that city. During consultations with the Egyptian archivists and priests, Solon learned of the existence of ancient texts that dated back to a remote and distant past, a past of which the Greeks had no conception.

The Egyptian priests described to Solon the occurrence of a great cataclysm. They explained that suddenly the Earth moved and the heavens shifted, and there was great destruction and chaos all over the world. They told of how the Egyptian lands had come through that time suffering less destruction than most. Therefore, in Egypt records had been preserved of the ancient times long ago. They went on to describe a great civilization that had once ruled over most of the world. The people of this truly ancient civilization excelled in culture, art and technology. This was the mighty and powerful Atlantic empire that ruled the world for ages, yet came to destruction by her own hand. Atlantis, her history and her people were swallowed up by the waters and ceased to exist upon the Earth.

It is not only through Plato, who lived between 427 and 347 B.C., that the Atlantis legend comes down to us today. Legends of a great flood and the destruction of an advanced civilization are common to the oral traditions of many tribal peoples all over the world. Within the last two centuries, volumes have been written on the subject. It has inspired historians, archaeologists, geologists, researchers of all kinds and various metaphysicians. Ask anyone you meet, and chances are that they are familiar with the story. However, most people consider it to be just that and nothing more. It is generally held to be myth, story and legend.

Some say we prearrange our own life experience according to the law of karma. Some say we have unseen guidance along the way, and some say that we are the illusion and that the *Spirit world* is the reality. I believe there are forces around us that we can't understand because we are generally unaware of their presence. It seems as though such forces in my Life have brought me to become involved in what I call the Atlantis connection. A few years ago I began receiving information concerning Atlantis from a highly evolved spiritual entity who lived during each of the three ages of Atlantean culture. This highly evolved spiritual being brings an important message for all people at this point in time.

Tiagorrah says that now is the time for all peoples to return to the ways of the Law of One. Due to the new and revealing information I have received from Tiagorrah, my concepts of time, space, and the history of mankind have been drastically altered. This is not just another book about Atlantis.

I have been guided, perhaps driven, to produce this book, because the knowledge and information it contains directly relate to what is happening in the present time within our own society. It is extremely important for people to realize that, in essence, history is repeating itself. According to Tiagorrah, *That which brought about the destruction of Atlantis is that which tears at the core of present society, and is the force that leads us to similar experience.*

It is vital that we wake up and acknowledge where we are heading, so that we can effect positive changes within ourselves and the world around us. Only by doing so will we be able to avoid imminent catastrophe and bring about a better world with a brighter future.

Since my arrival in Sedona, I have seen the evolution of this book take place. I have experienced the invisible hand of Spirit, moving myself and the project to completion. I have trusted that Spirit guides me and will continue to do so as I begin the work of promoting this book.

*You will come into the circle and take your part in the spiritual work toward the reintroduction of One Law consciousness into the world at this time.**

Apparently I don't have much of a choice in the matter. The purpose is to reach as many people as possible with this information. Not only does it reveal where our problems lie and what changes need to be made, it also explains how we can bring about these changes. It speaks about the Law of

*Tiagorrah breaks in from time to time, so his comments will appear in italics.

One, Tiagorrah's extremely important message for all of mankind today.

Throughout the writing of this book and during the time it has taken to compile this information, I have become more familiar with Tiagorrah. He tends to say a great deal while utilizing a minimum of words. You can't speed-read through his messages and understand what he is saying, so take your time and think about it. It's okay to read something over again and think about it for a minute before going on. He insisted that I capitalize certain words when transcribing the information for this book. He related this to me one day, saying

*There are certain things which, under the Law of One, are held sacred. You must always honor such things when referring to same in the written word. Such things are Life, Love, Earth and Spirit. Life is the great gift of the Creator; Love is the greatest force in the universe; the Earth is our mother; and Spirit is within and without all things.*

What a wonderful idea to honor these things in this way! Tiagorrah says that people did this back in early Atlantean times, and that we should be doing it today, teaching this in schools. When people ask why we capitalize these words, then it can be explained that they are sacred words and why they are so.

*Below our feet is the Earth, above our heads is*

*the realm of Spirit. Everywhere we go we must honor Life and carry Love within our hearts. This One Law concept finds acceptance and adoption when introduced to others. These will surely comprehend its significance, for soul memory of same will have been stirred within them.*

These are the four points on the circle, which represents the Law of One. This is a big part of what the book is all about. Therefore, I now present the following information as imparted by Tiagorrah of Poseidon: *And we shall leave the reader to make the determination as to whether this information is valid and useful in the individual sense and, ultimately, to the entire human collective.*

—W. T. Samsel

# Beginnings

In 1988 I was living in a typical St. Louis suburb. During this period I took over as supervisor of the second shift at the factory where I worked. I moved up from my old '67 Dodge to an '81 Buick Riviera, and moved out of a small dilapidated house into a more modern apartment in a better part of the city—a typical case of pursuing the American dream. At that time I was working hard, keeping with the program, and expecting to "get somewhere" as a result.

One fine Saturday morning I was sitting on the living room sofa, drinking my cup of coffee. The local *Riverfront Times* was lying on the coffee table, and I began casually leafing through it. Although I usually read the editorial page first, this time my attention was drawn to the entertainment section. It was then that my eyes fell upon a small box ad, which was as follows.

> Past-life regressions by Ruth, certified hypnotherapist. Private or group sessions available. Recorded on cassette tape for your continued enlightenment.

Now, this was something that was certainly different, and it just might prove to be interesting, too! Here was an alternative to the usual act of planting myself in front of the idiot box for an evening of sex, war, crime, violence, bloodshed and mind-numbing commercial advertisements. As I started to tear the little ad from the newspaper, something seemed to click inside my head. It was then that the whisper of a thought went drifting across my mind. It was as though I heard a soft voice saying, *This is something which may affect and bring change to the experience.*

Seeming to come from out of nowhere, the thought was there for only an instant and then it was gone. I paused and thought about it for a moment, but then shrugged it off, got up from the sofa and went about my way. Walking past the kitchen table, I tossed down the little piece of paper and wound up forgetting all about it . . . until later on.

One day a friend of mine happened to notice the

paper, which was lying on the floor at that point. She commented on the fact that she had been to visit Ruth for a past-life regression, and asked if I was planning to go. I admitted to having thought about it, but more for the purpose of entertainment than because I actually believed in the concept of reincarnation. I had always had a sense that other realities certainly exist, but I had never really delved into the realm of the supernatural. To this my friend replied, "There's nothing supernatural about it." She went into accounts of Spirit phenomena and strange occurrences, and proceeded to outline all things metaphysical in nature. She told me that Ruth is a wonderful person who's really good at what she does. She also suggested that I read a book or two before making the appointment.

Acting on her advice, I first read, *Here and Hereafter* by Ruth Montgomery. It dealt with belief in reincarnation, the continuance of the soul and Spirit communications through what is known as automatic writing. The next book I read was about Edgar Cayce, "the sleeping prophet," which also concerned communication from the Spirit realm. More books were to follow. I came upon each one of them in an extraordinary manner, as if they were being presented to me or as if I were being directed to them somehow. Well, this new information seemed to strike a chord somewhere deep inside me. I went from holding just a mild interest to having an awakened curiosity. This was all starting to get interesting!

I've always felt that there is more to Life and to being alive than merely what we perceive as reality. There has got to be something much greater, beyond what we perceive and accept as the three-dimensional world around us. All this information certainly seemed to ring true for me. It seemed much more natural, and made much more sense, than anything I had come to understand through my early Christian upbringing, yet I found that it enhanced the Christian teachings rather than detracted from them. I had a strange sense that perhaps some unseen guidance might be attempting to attract my attention. I had the feeling of a presence somewhere near, and that I was being drawn to learn more.

I was working at the time in a small plastics factory, which employed about a hundred people. They manufactured magnetic visual aids. In other words, they produced rubber magnets and magnetic boards. The second shift ran from three in the afternoon until midnight, and I was the second-shift supervisor.

I arrived at work one day to find everyone running around like chickens with their heads cut off. Machines were malfunctioning, orders were running way behind and too many people had called in sick. It looked like it was going to be one of those days. Fortunately, things began to ease up and return to normal about halfway through the shift.

I sat down in my little cubicle in the center of the plant and prepared to catch up on some paperwork. I had forsaken sleep the night before in order to read one of those books I mentioned earlier. Feeling tired, I closed my eyes for only a moment.

The next thing I knew, I was in a different space and time! I was running down a very beautiful forest pathway. It was warm and sunny, and pleasant smells filled the air. As I trotted along the pathway, I became aware that I carried something in my right hand. It was a long, spearlike weapon of some sort, and I remember wondering why it was so very heavy. In fact, it soon became so heavy that I could hardly go on carrying it. Huffing and puffing, I came to a stop. First I felt a great frustration, and then the idea hit me — throw it away, get rid of it! So with all my strength, I raised the lance over my head and let it fly. At that very same instant I was startled awake by my right arm, which had just gone through the throwing motion! Blinking my eyes, I realized that I must have fallen asleep. I looked over at the clock on the wall and saw that it had been a matter of only a few minutes. I somehow had the knowingness that this little dream was really more of a message coming in, a sort of communication.

That night I experienced another strange dream, which involved a cousin who had died the previous year. In the dream he was seated at a student's desk in a classroom. I viewed him as though I were standing before him and the class. Other students occupied similar desks, and the room was full of people. My cousin held up a sheet of paper with a large letter A on it, gave me the thumbs-up sign and smiled. The next morning when I awoke, I was able to recall the dream quite vividly and remembered every detail. Was this communication from the Spirit world? Was this another message coming in? As I was thinking this over, another thought seemed to speak to me from out of nowhere.

*It may be that you will begin writing soon.*

I wondered just what that meant. It appeared that something a bit out of the ordinary had been initiated. It was as if a series of events were pointing me in this otherworldly direction. I remember thinking that perhaps it was time to go and visit Ruth. At that time I had no idea what I was in for!

# First Past-Life Regression

I was all set to undergo my first past-life regression. As it turned out, Ruth certainly was a wonderful person, and I took a liking to her immediately. She had me lie down on a big, fluffy couch and helped adjust the many pillows until I was comfortable. She explained that she would be using a motorized hypnotic aid known as the "hypno disc." This device resembled a small electric fan, in that an electric motor rotated a disc about twelve inches in diameter that was imprinted with a black-and-white spiral pattern. As it slowly rotated, the pattern appeared to draw inward toward the center, creating an optical illusion. At Ruth's request, I fixed my eyes on the rotating disc and listened to her voice as she spoke her instructions and slowly counted from one to ten.

I wanted this session to be a success, so I cooperated as best I could. I had never been hypnotized before and questioned whether I could be hypnotized at all. I didn't know what to expect; I had no idea what sort of experience this would turn out to be. When Ruth spoke the number ten, I looked into her eyes, and as I did, her face began to expand! As her face grew larger and larger, my eyes slowly closed and I was on my way.

The following is excerpted from a transcript of that past-life regression . . .

**You and I are going to be able to communicate and talk to each other even though you are in this deep state of consciousness. I want you to get used to talking to me now. Where are you?**

I'm questioning.

**Are you questioning where you are right now?**

[No reply.]

**Is there anyone there you are questioning?**

I don't know.

**What do you feel?**

I feel like I'm somewhere beyond the body. Something says "state of mind." It appears to be within, it must be within!

**Don't get frustrated with yourself. Look around you. What do you see?**

Could be a ball, a sphere or a planet. It's getting larger or I'm going into it. What is this place? Looks like a great big bump down there on the ground. This is really very strange!

**Describe it to me, no matter how strange it may seem.**

It's hard to see. There are lights down there, and something beyond, off in the distance. It looks like the sun is coming up. There's that bump down there.

**What is the bump? Can you get closer to it?**

I'm aware of people dressed in flowing robes. Many of them gather at the base of this huge mass. There are mountains on one side, and off in the distance is the light of dawn. I can make out structures and people moving around down there. Yes, this is definitely a city, but I can't make out exactly what they're . . .

**What are you doing?**

I'm just looking at it all, watching the people. I can see everything from here.

**So, are you in Spirit form rather than embodied?**

I can't make out what they're doing.

**Can you move in closer to them?**

One man is talking before a group of people. He's speaking and making gestures.

**He's addressing the people?**

He's speaking to this gathering of people. Some are listening to what he has to say, while others walk by and continue on their way. He's teaching at the foot of a great stepped mound. He's holding something brilliant in his right hand!

**Is this like an Indian mound?**

Yes, but these don't appear to be Indians. He's got a perfectly clear quartz crystal in his hand. That's what he's holding.

**Where do you think this is? What area? What part of the world?**

I can't tell that . . . but it's great; I can just hang here!

**You mean that at will, just by wanting to maneuver without mass, you can freely move about?**

Yes.

**Are you comfortable with what the people are doing there?**

They've come looking for knowledge.

**Are these people aware of you?**

No.

**But you are very much aware of them.**

Yes.

**Do you feel the need to communicate with them in any way?**

I'm not sure. I'm just watching them.

**Do you get the feeling that this is . . . even though you are not seeing all that could be affected or involved, do you have a feeling that there are more of them than you can see now?**

There's a whole planet full of them! I am floating over a huge city, and below me I can see a great stepped pyramid. It's a beautiful temple!

**You're at peace with what they're doing. You're aware that they just want to learn, and yet there's nothing you need to say to them. You're like a bystander.**

[Now Tiagorrah is responding:] *More as an observer.*

**Are you keeping some record or account of what you're observing?**

*Each carries within them their own record, yet the many make up the whole, and so I would question whether they exist in harmony together.*

**Why do you feel it is your position to see if they are in harmony?**

*It is my observation that they should exist in harmony and refuse to threaten.*

**Who is it that they would be threatening?**

*Each other.*

**What do you see as your purpose for observing all of this?**

*Acknowledgment. Completion.*

**The crystal that the one is holding, are you attracted to it?**

*It is a tool, it has certain properties.*

**You have a knowingness of that. How long do you have to observe them?**

*I still do.*

**How long have you been doing this?**

*A very long time.*

**Yes, you have. You just needed to know that. What have you concluded from your observations?**

*That they will do great harm to themselves.*

**What would you do to keep them from harming themselves?**

*I would simply remind them of that which they have forgotten.*

**When you become a part of them, taking on the human form to become one of them, and participate in their norm, do you feel inclined to give them that message?**

*Such would be the purpose. Though many believe only in what they choose to believe, there will be those who would listen. There will be those who would be drawn to the message.*

**Do you sense in your observation that this is a particular civilization you're looking at now?**

*It is truly ancient.*

**Because you focused in on the crystal and the stepped pyramid, do you have the feeling that this could be Lemuria or Atlantis?**

*This is Poseidon, the great capital city of Atlantis.*

**I want you to understand that in a regression, what you are actually doing is remembering. You are experiencing something that's in your memory bank, that has some sort of significance, some importance to you. So this place, this scene, is relevant to who you are. I want you to think about this scene that you targeted, that you went to. What is it that you feel you are learning here?**

*I observe the cycles of humanity.*

**When will you have observed and learned enough?**

*Soon.*

**If your experience here is to learn, to observe and understand, then many of the things that man has done for centuries upon this planet could be in total disagreement with who and what you are. It's like you were sent here to do this.**

I feel like I know this man.

**Which man?**

The one with the crystal in his hand.

My first experience with past-life regression had proved to be quite interesting. Once under hypnosis, I was amazed to find myself as a discarnate being in an unexpected and fantastic place.

The experience left me in a quandary, for it challenged my logical reasoning. Was I to believe that my Life force had its origins in some far-off solar system in outer space? That I have been experiencing lifetimes here on Earth ever since the days of Atlantis? That I am some kind of cosmic observer, here to take part in the human race in order to observe the cycles of humanity?

It would certainly have been a lot easier and more rational to explain the experience as a product of the imagination or something similar to a good old-fashioned daydream. Ruth, of course, expressed no doubt as to the validity of the information that came through. However, I just didn't know what to think, and wondered if there would ever be a way of verifying what had occurred.

I also questioned whether I had actually been under hypnosis, in an altered state. Thinking back over the session, I remembered being aware of lying on the couch, hearing the air conditioner kick on and off, and sounds floating in from the street. I had always assumed hypnosis to be a sleeplike state of unconsciousness, a dreamlike trance in which a person is unaware of sounds and sensations emanating from the physical world around him.

If I had not been in a trance state, then why had I not simply opened my eyes, sat up and asked for my money back? I remember not moving a single muscle throughout the entire experience. At the time, to have moved at all seemed as though it would have taken great strength and effort. During the session I was not at all concerned about the body; my focus was elsewhere. I was busy experiencing and evaluating the experience at the same time. It had been very much as though I was there and yet I wasn't — like I said earlier, a quandary.

I listened to the cassette recording of the session over and over and spent many hours in thought. Then one day, after listening once again to this tape, something strange took place. I had started writing notes and comments on a piece of paper, attempting to do some intense analysis, but was not making any headway. My mind kept wandering and I was unable to keep my thoughts focused on what I was doing. Then suddenly, words began flowing into my head just like a stream of water into a hole! I had to speed up my writing to keep up with the flow. I knew that if I couldn't keep up with it, I would lose it. This was my first communication from Tiagorrah by means of automatic writing.

*The rational mind will conflict over that from beyond the subconscious. The conscious mind believes only that which is perceived through the five physical senses. Those five senses relate only to the three dimensions of this plane of existence.*

*Therefore, anything which emanates from beyond those five senses or from beyond those three dimensions will be called into question or dismissed as nonreality. Much takes place around the physical being of which that being is unaware. When things such as these are detected through physical sensory input, it is only natural, within your limited dimensional experience, to question such occurrences. Acceptance comes with time and with knowledge; it comes through understanding.*

Well, now I had something else to sit and think about! Where did all *that* come from? Was it simply a creation of my imagination, or was it actually a communication in answer to my questioning? Had I truly experienced automatic writing, or was it merely a delusion? A week later, after going over the regression and the "channeled" message again and again, I was still unable to draw any firm conclusions. Weary of contemplation, I decided to put it out of my mind, and instead lie down to meditate. It wasn't very long before I became aware of a brilliant purple light—there, in the vision of my closed eyes! It moved around, pulsing in shape and intensity. Then words started to flow into my consciousness . . .

*Know that we have made the connection, the contact, so to speak. Know that soon a great abundance of knowledge and understanding shall come into the experience.*

*The pathway ahead is one of discovery, of contemplation, analysis and trust. You will come into the circle and take your part in the spiritual work toward the reintroduction of One Law consciousness into the world at this time. Know that meditation rather than critical analysis would be more productive.*

# GETTING ACQUAINTED

The following are excerpts from a transcript of the first verbal channeling of information from Tiagorrah. This took place on August 28, 1988. I had been practicing meditation with more regularity, choosing to do so every night after getting home from work. On that particular night I went into a very deep state of meditation, and once again words began to flow into my awareness. I found myself listening to the flow of information, and then speaking the words aloud as they came in.

*You wish to know, to understand what is taking place in the experience. This, and the reason for same, relate to the purpose of being at this time and place. You must allow your own light to shine through, to guide you along the pathway. You will question the words which come through to you now. Know that the key is to learn to trust that which comes forth at this time.*

It seemed as though I was standing back, disconnecting myself, and thus allowing the flow of words to come through. There was a very strong sense of an energy, a presence, in very close proximity. It was a very strange sensation in that there was a familiarity to this energy, this presence. As though aware of my thoughts, the flow continued.

*I have spoken to you many times in the past, before you became aware. As your awareness grows, I will speak to you more often and in many ways. This will all be new to you, but there will be many such things you will learn. Know that I have and will always walk with you.*

I remember wondering if this was valid communication, or merely a product of my imagination. Again, seeming to sense my thought, the flow went on . . .

*At this moment you do question this communication, though you have called upon the presence which now speaks through you. I am that of the small voice within, that force which helps to guide you. I am that which is many ages in age and many names in being. Know this one as Tiagorrah of the city of Poseidon.*

Simply forming a question in thought seemed to trigger a flow of information in response. Was this truly a telepathic communication? As I focused my attention on some notes I had written concerning my new experiences, the answer came back . . .

*Much knowledge I shall impart to you for you to bring into being. This all has a purpose. It will continue, it will grow and be nurtured. In time you will understand.*

These few sentences comprised my first verbal channeling of Tiagorrah. It was rather short and sweet, but it was also very interesting.

I soon found myself being drawn to crystals and stones of many different kinds. I began using crystals as the focal point in my meditation. I would arrange a crystal against a candle flame in such a way as to reflect the most brilliant spectrum of color through that crystal. I found this produced a very peaceful and soothing dance of light upon which to focus.

I set up a little altar for my new meditation tools. This consisted of a small folding table draped with a blue-velvet fabric, upon which I placed a candle, an incense burner, some sage, an abalone shell and my few crystals and stones.

My attraction to crystals and stones grew stronger, and there were certain ones to which I was drawn. Learning about them and using them in my meditation seemed easy and perfectly natural. I remember one incident involving a deep purple stone I had noticed in a little New Age shop. I had an intense desire to obtain that particular stone, although at the time I had no idea why. The only reason I didn't go ahead and get it then was because I didn't have enough money with me. Later that evening, I went into meditation and asked Tiagorrah about this stone. Tiagorrah provided the following . . .

*Know the deep purple ray as that which reflects spiritual awakening, enlightenment and understanding, that which helps one understand one's Life's purpose, the reasons for Life's lessons. This ray can reduce negative thoughts and emotions, as it can promote positive thoughts and actions. It can protect one against hurt and disappointment in this world. This ray is of deep vibration, and so is good for penetrating to the deeper realms of meditation. Know this ray.*

I had an intense attraction to that stone as I gazed at it in the display case that day. It turned out to be sugilite and, according to Tiagorrah, was just the stone for my need at the time. Could it have been that my attraction to that particular stone was actually more of a direction to it by Tiagorrah?

A few days later I acquired the stone and carried it around in my pocket wherever I went. When I lay down to meditate, I would place it on my third-eye chakra. Crystals, stones and other "medicine" objects soon began to come into my Life in many different ways. I would come to utilize them in my future work; however, I didn't know this at the time. A lot had taken place and great deal more would happen in the future. Although I didn't know the what, how, why or when of it, I knew it would certainly be interesting!

# TIAGORRAH OF POSEIDON

What is the source of the information, the communication I receive in this otherworldly manner? What is the nature of the spiritual entity who was once Tiagorrah of Poseidon? What is the purpose of this "Atlantis connection?" These are questions I asked myself over and over again in those early days.

Spirit communication, or what is commonly referred to as channeling, can be described as the transference of information from the nonphysical realm to the physical world, from the nonmaterial to the material. This is communication across what we refer to as the space-time continuum. It is accomplished through a sort of telepathic focus or fine-tuning on the part of both the sender and the receiver. Tiagorrah initiated the projection of ancient knowledge and higher consciousness across the space-time continuum from the Spirit realm. This he refers to as the Project. I refer to it as the Atlantis connection. It is for the purpose of reintroducing One Law consciousness into our troubled world in the here and now.

I would have to describe Tiagorrah as a spiritual consciousness, a highly evolved Spirit being who brings an enormous understanding of what he refers to as the Law of One. This is the great universal law of unity, of the interconnection of all things. This being lived during each of the three ages of Atlantean history, and retains memory of all three Atlantean incarnations in order to communicate that knowledge to a reception point in the here and now. I am that reception point.

This entity points to the star system Sirius in reference to origin, and had been among those of the star system Pleiades before first taking physical form as Tiagorrah the Atlantean.

*This being, and others, did attend to duties upon the bridge of a Pleiadian spacecraft long ago. The focus of our attention was the blue planet Terra, above which we did maintain orbital seating at the time.*

Tiagorrah has provided no further information

about this or any other pre-Atlantean manifestation.

During the Lemurian/early Atlantic age, Tiagorrah was born as Thaeles, the son of Armadus, the Earth Keeper, and Thesteelae, a ceremonial priestess. Accordingly, Tiagorrah was educated under the One Law and accepted into the priesthood. He became a high priest, residing in the Temple of the One Law in the heart of Atlantia. During his 900-year lifespan, Thaeles experienced the arrival of extraterrestrial relations, which at the time heralded the beginning of a new age for Atlantis. He lived during the period of progress, technology and transition initiated by Zeus, Poseidon and Ra.

Thaeles was one of the vocal opposition against the walled encirclement or enclosure of the Atlantia land proposed by Poseidon. He actively opposed many of Poseidon's manipulations of Atlantia, the Atlantean people and, most importantly, the One Law. When Poseidon installed his own descendants as rulers over Atlantean government, Thaeles and other priests went out from Atlantis under the Order of the Word. They sought to preserve One Law consciousness from a new religious movement, which manifested as the Temple of the Sun.

During the second Atlantean age Tiagorrah was born of Cephestes, high priest of the Temple of One, and Lumina, daughter of Theositus-Ra, a leading grower and merchant on the isle of Og. In his childhood Tiagorrah attended services and ceremonies at the Temple of the One Law in the city of Poseidon. There he was educated and accepted into the priesthood.

Tiagorrah was involved in airplane design and technology during the second Atlantean age. His fascination with flight and machines of the air led him to become an aerodynamic engineer. He spent many years working in the research and development department at the Temple of Flight in the city of Poseidon. While in residence there, he devoted time to important projects concerning the evolution of Atlantean aircraft designs. Tiagorrah was also involved with educational activities at that temple. This was a period of rapid growth and progress in Atlantean aircraft technology.

Tiagorrah disagreed with the political and societal attitudes and tendencies surfacing in Poseidon at that time. Government and the military grew more deeply involved in research and development programs. The military envisioned fleets of airships with great destructive capabilities. These were to be utilized by Atlantis against less developed peoples in order for her to progress and expand as the dominant world power. This went against the principles of the Law of One.

Tiagorrah's Love and enthusiasm for participation in the progress and evolution of aeronautics began to decline and was lost. Because of this, Tiagorrah resigned from work at the Temple of Flight. His resignation from a high position at the temple came to the Atlantean public's attention. Tiagorrah was well-known as the designer of what at the time was Atlantis' largest transport aircraft. When one of Atlantis' top design engineers resigned his position, it became the news of the day. Therefore, his statement of resignation stirred public debate. After his departure from the aeronautics field, he sought refuge at the Temple of the One Law. There he remained and performed his greatest work. He became a high priest, ceremonial leader, teacher, author and advocate.

Tiagorrah was both praised and criticized by many Atlanteans for his stand that crystal technology must not be utilized in a destructive manner or as a power source for weapons then being developed that would be turned against other civilizations. Tiagorrah believed that aggressive acts of expansionism would promote a world-view of Atlantis as a threat and enemy. It would create resentment, resistance and conflict.

Tiagorrah spoke of a policy of mutual respect, of offering assistance and guidance and promoting intercultural learning and understanding. He spoke of the teachings of the Law of One. To act from this consciousness would ensure a world-view of Atlantis as friend, benefactor and world leader.

*The political powers at the time felt that Atlantis' great wealth and power, her technology and military might, constituted her right to global domination. Many in government and industry saw unlimited growth for Atlantis, regardless of the means through which such growth would be accomplished. These maintained that the planet Terra, under Atlantean rule, would be a place of peace and prosperity for all of mankind. While debate continued, Atlantis went on with her agenda and research and development intensified. Improvement of crystal technology and weaponry went forward, and Atlantean expansionism accelerated.*

As a high priest of the Temple of the One Law, Tiagorrah was an outspoken advocate of One Law principles. He spoke publicly in Poseidon and other Atlantean cities, and he also produced many writings. As he spoke out in advocacy of the One Law, so too did he speak out against the Sons of Belial at a time when these held great power and influence throughout the land. Atlantis was then dealing with conflict in what is now India and Tibet. It seems the indigenous people didn't approve of a planned buildup of Atlantean military forces in the area, anticipating an Atlantean expansion that would include China.

Tiagorrah came to be seen as a threat by the Sons of Belial and powerful people in government and industry. When he began to target individuals who occupied the highest echelons of power, it became necessary for them to remove the threat. It was arranged that Tiagorrah be discredited and suspended from his duties at the One Temple. Under the Order of the Word, he was sent to the far land we now know as Egypt, where he continued to teach the One Law to the people of that general area.

Tiagorrah later journeyed to the Americas, where he favored association with the natural environment and the native peoples, the ancient ancestors of peoples such as the Anasazi, Hopi, Aztecs, Mayans and Olmecs. During his later years, Tiagorrah experienced visions of a far-distant future on the Earth, a time when mankind would completely abandon the Law of One. Tiagorrah knew then that the time would come when the reintroduction of One Law consciousness would be of paramount importance. That time is now.

*While this entity conducted One Law teachings in the land now known as the Four Corners region of the United States, Atlantis did continue her expansionist agenda. She did instigate conflict and war, until causing the event of the second great cataclysm to take place.*

During the late Atlantic age Tiagorrah again

experienced incarnation as an Atlantean. Of that experience, he relates that it followed a course very similar to the two previously described. Tiagorrah's three Atlantean lifetimes paralleled each other in several ways. He was born into a family of priests and priestesses of the One Law; he attained the high priesthood at the Temple of the One Law; then became a political, social and spiritual activist, opposing the manipulation of the One Law; and went out from Atlantis to teach and preserve the One Law.

*In such ways and others do this entity's Atlantean experiences mirror each other.*

When Tiagorrah teaches about the cycles of humanity, he speaks with the knowledge and experience of all three physical Atlantean manifestations. That the reintroduction of One Law consciousness at present is the full thrust of this being's intent is understandable. Also apparent should be the severity of the present situation and the greatness of the need for this Project, which is the Atlantis connection.

# Atlantean Creation Story

*I would speak at this time as concerns early Atlantean creation beliefs, as were handed down from generation to generation in those ages past. It happened that from the vast, unformed mass of elements came that which did form the order of the universe. This Creator brought forth light and energy to fashion the stars and planets. Creator did then bring forth light beings like Itself. These were emitted outward from Its being. Then the Creator brought forth Life, sexuality and reproduction.*

*The Earth was created and atmosphere was formed around her. Then the Earth did come alive and Life came to be upon her. Through time did these things occur and evolve, as was intended.*

*Then it happened that lightbeings became involved in the Earth and the Life thereupon. The Creator then did cause to develop a physical vehicle for lightbeings to inhabit in the Earth-plane experience.*

*The Creator did bring about modern man for the karmic progression of lightbeings through the density of the physical world. Man did increase in number to develop culture and civilization. They were first in the Lemurian land, and then the Atlantean. So were the teachings in those times past.*

# RECORDED HISTORY AND THE CYCLES OF HUMANITY

*I would speak at this time concerning the recorded history of mankind, that which is known to you through your own experience and learning. Know that such as does exist of recorded history refers backward in time only 5000 years from present, such as that which did take place approximately 3000 years before the birth of the Christ upon this Earth.*

*Of the times before this no records exist, and to your general knowledge only legend and myth survive. Knowledge of distant times past is only that which is assumed from the fragmented evidence resultant of mankind's diggings in the Earth. This knowledge is lost with the passage of time and the effects of atmospheric and geologic conditions. Know that in the physical, material world 10,000 years' passage of time has the effect of purification, a cleansing, upon and within the Earth. Such a span of time leaves little trace of those who came before. Much of mankind's history is lost to his knowledge and understanding this day.*

I investigated Tiagorrah's reference to 3000 B.C. as being the farthest point back in time to which recorded history can be traced. Looking into the histories of Egypt, China and India, I found that date to be fairly accurate.

Although it is accepted that the roots of the Egyptian civilization trail back about 9000 years, recorded events date back only 5000 years. Upper Egypt conquered Lower Egypt around 3000 B.C. Menes became the first king of a united Egypt and founded the city of Memphis around 2900 B.C. The Step Pyramid, said to be the oldest pyramid, was built by King Djoser and his chief architect, Imhotep, around 2630 B.C.

In China the legendary Emperor Yu, the first ruler of the Hsia Dynasty, founded the dynastic system in the twenty-third century B.C. The Bronze Age Shang Dynasty ruled from approximately 1500 to 1000 B.C. The Chinese classical age, the age of Confucius and Buddha, began during the sixth century B.C.

In India evidence indicates that a neolithic village culture existed there 5000 years ago. India's actual recorded history dates back to approximately 1500 B.C. The Vedic hymns are believed to have been written around that time. Hindu religion evolved between 900 and 550 B.C.

*I would speak now concerning Solon of Athens and that which came to his experience in the land of Egypt. Egyptian priests and archivists did speak to Solon of ancient records and texts, histories which told of a far-distant antediluvian past. These records told of the great civilization of Atlantis and her rule over vast portions of the Earth. Such records did indeed truly exist. Many known at that time were gathered and kept stored within the great library of Alexandria. Those which were preserved within this depository were lost to mankind with its destruction.*

*At this time there exists no physical evidence in your experience to support that such records did ever exist. If such records as these were to become available to the knowledge of present experience, then surely would mankind's understanding and perception of the past find radical revision.*

*The perception of mankind is such that time is comprehended as being linear in nature. Thus events are seen to occur upon a single linear con-*

*tinuum. Therefore, it is accepted that it took nearly 40,000 years for modern man to progress from cave dweller to astronaut. This is a misconception born out of limited perception.*

*The reason for this is that the eyes of man's perception cannot see far enough back in time. If such were possible, then it would be acknowledged that time is cyclic rather than linear, that mankind's collective experience is governed by karmic cycles. Then you would understand that which I refer to as the cycles of humanity. Such are the cycles of the incarnate whole.*

*That mankind has had ample time to develop, not merely once, but several times, advanced civilizations that were destroyed through war and natural means, is a difficult concept for many to accept. There is much that lies just beyond your eyes' vision through the past. Know that the area at the site which is now known as Giza in Egypt was under Atlantean influence up until 12,000 years ago. That which is known this day as the Sphinx was begun in construction over 15,000 years ago. The temple at its feet was constructed 14,000 years ago from present, when that land was green with Life. The Sphinx has now begun to reveal its long-held secrets to those with the openness of mind to understand the language through which it communicates.*

*Know that modern man's influence in the Earth*

*dates back 80,000 years in time. Creator had taken from the animal world and there had evolved a perfected vehicle for lightbeings to inhabit through karmic cycles of growth and experience on the Earth plane.*

Tiagorrah states that God created modern man, what he calls the perfected vehicle, through a series of gradual evolutionary stages. Therefore, it appears that *both* the creationists and the evolutionists are correct!

*Although the earlier Neanderthal beings were not nearly the brutal, savage beasts of your present conception, they yet were not the intended perfected vehicle. The first modern human beings came into the Earth in the land of Mu, that which was then Lemuria, 80,000 years ago. They did also appear 70,000 years past in the land which would be Atlantis. From that place they did spread to what would be Africa, and then yet to other parts of the Earth.*

Tiagorrah states that modern man appeared in Lemuria 80,000 years ago and in Atlantis, 70,000 years ago. This pushes modern man back twice as far as contemporary estimates. Tiagorrah states that the Neanderthals, who existed before modern man, were not yet the intended "vehicle." Modern man's appearance, then, signaled the decline of the Neanderthal. Africa is currently accepted as the cradle of mankind, and it is estimated that modern man drove out the Neanderthal approximately 40,000 years ago.

*Modern man, the perfected vehicle, did appear in the Atlantean land. They did experience growth and learning and did develop culture and civilization. This was a period when early Atlanteans were a very tribal people. These were the times of the sacred Earth of that which was Atlantia, or the sacred center of Atlantis.*

*There were those people who gathered in small township communities, while others built large cities. There were many who chose to remain nomadic, following the Earth cycles and rhythms like their four-legged and winged relations. There were the northern, southern, eastern and western tribes. During this time Atlantis was ruled by a council of elders chosen by the various peoples. All did live in peace under the Law of One, and so there was peace and harmony and a purely spiritual way of Life.*

Tiagorrah states that the people grew and developed culture and civilization in Atlantis over a period of 12,000 years. According to him, these early Atlanteans were a tribal people ruled by a council of elders. They shared a common holy ground and a central temple. Some of these people built cities, while some chose to remain close to the Earth. This sounds very much like a description of Native Americans. What Tiagorrah describes here is a socially and spiritually advanced culture similar to the Native American culture of our understanding.

*This early age of Atlantean history did last for 12,000 years, until the day when our relatives from the Pleiades did enter into our experience nearly 60,000 years ago. At that time did Poseidon come to have great influence in Atlantis, and the sacred center, Atlantia, did begin to evolve into that which would be the city of Poseidon. With the rule of Poseidon there began the royal lineage of kings and queens, who ruled over the Atlantean land for over 8000 years.*

*Know that these things of which I have spoken did take place before that which I have referred to as the first destruction. This was the great shifting of the Earth upon its axis 50,000 years ago, which did destroy the Lemurian land. Atlantis did survive that destruction, but the great island did break into several, and much of culture and civilization was lost.*

*Know that since man's beginnings on the Earth, there have been several cycles of experience through which the collective human species has passed. The first cycle of man's experience was that of the Lemurian. During that time he did come to rise in the land of Atlantis as well. For a time, both lands and peoples did exist on the Earth, before the event of the first destruction.*

*The next turn of the wheel did give rise to the great and powerful Atlantean empire, a civilization which has yet to be equalled. This did come to have great influence over much of the Earth. Ultimately, there came a period of many wars, and during the greatest of these, Atlantis was destroyed by her own hand and the empire crumbled. This was the age of the great Atlantic empire.*

*The next age could be termed the lesser, or late, Atlantic age. The Atlantic isles had been reduced considerably. The few survivors did return to the Law of One and walk the good road for a time. They did rebuild to a degree. Our extraterrestrial relations did withdraw from mankind's experience. Once again Atlantis grew arrogant and powerful, and did attempt to reestablish itself as a world power. Came then the destruction which did wipe away all trace of these people and their culture, when again the Earth did shift upon her axis. This was the third great cataclysm.*

*Know that the age in which your people dwell at present is that of the fourth age, or cycle. It is a cycle that has grown nearly devoid of the One Law. It is a dark cycle for mankind and the Earth, a time of social and economic upheaval, war and suffering. It is an age wherein the powers of greed and corruption are dominant. At the end of this cycle man will suffer cataclysm by his own hand and through upheavals upon and within the Earth. Then will begin that of the fifth age of man upon the Earth.*

*Know that there do exist the cycles of the vast universe. There are the cycles of the mother, Earth. Upon the Earth there are the cycles of collective humanity, within which are the cycles of man's civilizations. Interwoven within these are the cycles of the individual beings. All is in order, all is interconnected, and so is the Law of One. I have no more of which to speak at this time.*

This is Tiagorrah's account of five ages through which mankind has progressed on the Earth. These are what Tiagorrah refers to as the cycles of humanity. According to this information, man has developed technological civilizations not once, but several times in the past. These civilizations existed ages before recorded history as we know it today. The Greek writer Hesiod lived during the seventh century B.C., more than 2500 years ago. In his writings, Hesiod also described five distinct ages of mankind. I excerpt Hesiod's account as follows.

> The immortals made a golden race of mortal men. These existed at a time when Cronus was king in heaven. They lived without toil or trouble. Old age did not come upon them. The fertile land of its own accord

bore fruit ungrudgingly and in great abundance. They did, in peace and harmony, manage their affairs, rich in flocks and beloved by the gods. Then the Earth covered over this race of men.

The immortals made a second race. This race was of silver, and these grew unlike the others, both physically and mentally. These grew to be arrogant and selfish. The Earth covered over this race, too.

Father Zeus then made a new race of men, the third, of bronze, and not at all like the ones of silver. These became terrible and mighty because of their spears of ash. Great was their might, and unconquerable hands grew upon the strong limbs which stretched forth from their body. When these came to be destroyed by their own hand, they went down into the chill dark of Hades.

When the Earth covered over this race too, again did Zeus, the son of Cronus, make still another race, the fourth race of men upon the nourishing Earth. These dwelt at the end of the Earth and inhabited the small islands by the deep, swirling ocean. Far-seeing Zeus made still another race of men. Oh, that I were not a part of this fifth world! Now indeed the race is of iron, for they never cease from toil and woe by day nor from thieves in the night. They grow old very quickly. They find faults with all others. They do not know respect for men or for gods, for their own might is right. No esteem will be held for those who are just and good, but rather men praise the arrogance and evil of the wicked.

Such is Hesiod's account of the five ages of man

in Greek mythology. Comparing the information of Tiagorrah with that of Hesiod reveals many similarities. After reading through both several times, I have come to the conclusion that the first two worlds of Hesiod's description must have existed at the same time and suffered the same violent cataclysm.

"Immortal" is defined in Webster's dictionary as "being without end." Was the Pleiadians' great longevity translated by the Greeks as immortality? Hesiod states that the immortals made a golden race of mortal men" and then "the immortals made a second race." Therefore, according to Hesiod, beings without end created gold and silver races of men. Both of these races were then "covered over." He uses the same sentence twice. "The Earth covered over this race" and then "the Earth covered over this race, too."

I believe Hesiod was saying that both races existed at the same time and that both experienced the same destructive cataclysm.

According to Tiagorrah, both Lemuria and the early Atlanteans existed at the same time, before the first destruction. Hesiod's first two races could very well represent Lemuria and Atlantis before the Earth shift. Therefore I combine Hesiod's first two races and consider that these experienced the same destruction.

| | HESIOD | TIAGORRAH |
|---|---|---|
| | *gold* | *Lemuria/early Atlantic* |
| **First Cataclysm** | | |
| | *silver* | *Atlantean empire* |
| **Second Cataclysm** | | |
| | *bronze* | *Late Atlantic* |
| **Third Cataclysm** | | |
| | *iron* | *Modern age* |

If Hesiod's first two races existed at the same time and experienced the same destruction, then it follows that his third, fourth and fifth ages would move up, the third becoming the silver race, the fourth becoming the bronze race, and the fifth becoming the iron race.

After his description of the first two races, Hesiod goes on to state that "Father Zeus then made a new race of men" and that "this terrible race was destroyed by their own hand." Now, this race, according to my chart, coincides with the Atlantean empire, according to Tiagorrah. Everything seems to fit rather neatly into place. Hesiod's fourth race becomes the bronze race on my list, and it coincides with Tiagorrah's late Atlantic period. Hesiod relates little about this race, and nothing about a cataclysmic occurrence. He simply states that they "lived at the ends of the Earth and on the islands by the deep ocean." This corresponds to Tiagorrah's late Atlantic age. According to Tiagorrah, there occurred another Earth axial tilt. This was the third destruction, which brought that age to a close. Finally, Hesiod's fifth race becomes the iron race, coinciding with the modern age on Tiagorrah's list.

It is interesting to note that in Hesiod's writing, "Father Zeus" is credited with the creation of two races of man. According to Tiagorrah, Zeus was the overseer of his people's operations and involvement in the Earth. Ages afterward, by Hesiod's time, Zeus had evolved into a god in every sense of the word. This god held the power of creation and the ability to manipulate the Earth and men. Tiagorrah suggests that when we read the word *race* in Hesiod's account, we should define its meaning as *association,* or *presence.* Thus Zeus made another *association* or *presence* among men, a truer meaning behind the words.

Comparison of Tiagorrah's information and that of Hesiod reveals a four-age scenario. Ovid, a Roman poet, writing some several hundred years after Hesiod, also describes four ages of man in the Earth. Again, Ovid describes gold, silver, bronze and iron races of men. Legends of the Native American Hopi tribe describe four ages or races of men on the Earth, too. This is a common theme that shows up in several other cultures in the past and at present.

# Our Relations from the Stars

*I would speak at this time concerning those who came from far-distant places in the vast universe, from the star systems known this day as the Pleiades, Arcturus, Orion, Sirius and Andromeda. These as well as others did gather to witness the first steps of infant humanity. From the heavens came Titans to the Earth. Great distances they traveled for the purpose of observation. These had come to study the metamorphosis which was then taking place here. This was for the purpose of furthering their understanding of themselves, the universe, and the All That Is. Some chose the path of nonintervention, while others did choose to involve themselves. So came these extraterrestrial relations, and they did settle into their orbital seatings far above the Earth.*

*I would now describe these beings and certain aspects of their involvement in mankind's experience. Know that among these relations there were the directors of various geologic, biologic, meteorologic and oceanic research operations. There were also priests whose purpose was to study the spiritual aspects of mankind's progression then. Logistically, these programs did require a vast technical and material support network. This involved communications, supply, medical and security equipment and personnel.*

*Cronos* the Sirian, and his assistant Ree*, the Pleiadian geologist, held ultimate authority over all operations involved in the Titan project. Cronos had been appointed to this position under the authority of a corporation of academic and entrepreneurial interests. Know this as the Titan Group. This was a joint collaboration between the Pleiadians and those from Orion, Sirius and Arcturus. These worked under the supervision of Pleiadian government authorities. In actuality, the Pleiadian High Council relied heavily on periodic progress reports furnished by Cronos, forwarded through the Titan project headquarters, which was located at their*

---

*These are Tiagorrah's spellings.

*base on Mars. Oceanos and Ethis were two aspects of the Titan project which alone required a combined work force of over 6000 personnel.*

*Understand that Oshenos* refers to oceanographic study, or marine biology, and Ethis relates to the study of atmospherics, or meteorology. Iperenos and Iyea were the command and logistical personnel who did oversee all modes of transportation. They brought in Helios and Selee*, technical engineers who conducted the operation and supervised maintenance of the great ships. Cronos had divided the land of Lemuria and did appoint such others to direct operations in the various sections. Cronos held authority for thousands of years. Thus it was that the progression of man in the Lemurian land came to be the focus of the Titan observation and research project long ago.*

*I would speak now as concerns a great conflict which arose between these relations. For over time there did develop an internal struggle for power and control between the elements involved. Cronos and his program directors did focus upon human development taking place in the Lemurian land as well as events taking place there. Eventually they became aware of man's emergence and progression in the Atlantean land. They did, however, continue*

---

*Tiagorrah's spellings.

*to maintain their focus on the Lemurians, and would not transfer effort or attention to the Atlanteans. They viewed the Lemurians as the advanced race, of greater spiritual awareness and understanding, of a higher vibration, more in tune with the All That Is.*

*There were certain elements involved in the project who also became aware of the progress of man in Atlantis and were impressed with Atlantean inventiveness and creativity. These were most interested in that of the Atlanteans' propensity toward technological development. They wanted to expand the operation and to divert those resources which would make for Atlantean inclusion. These did feel that the Titan operation was far too vast in size and too focused in one area of the globe. They did maintain that the operation was inefficient, excessive and expensive. These did also maintain that, under their monitoring, the same number of personnel, or less, could encompass the Earth's sphere with greater efficiency and effectiveness. By this time Cronos and the others were well into their programs, concentrated upon the Lemurian experience. These thought little of the Atlanteans. From such seed did the conflict arise between the elements involved therein.*

*So Cronos came to believe that certain personnel were involved in efforts to undermine his authority.*

*His suspicions centered on the Pleiadian security force and did result in a procession of command personnel being brought in by Ree. Cronos distrusted them all. He did in turn accuse them of conspiracy, strip them of their authority and imprison them. Thus divisions between both elements grew into argument and confrontation. Through ego and distrust did the authority of the one come to challenge the authority of the other. Ree then referred to the higher authority of the Pleiadian High Council. These did intervene, and arrangements were made to bring in Zeus and transfer him to "Earth ground" in secret. When the Pleiadian Council did order Cronos to release the imprisoned officers, these and others joined with Zeus against him. The one would not relinquish authority to the other. This led to open conflict. And so it was by force that Zeus did come into control.*

*At this time did relations from the star system Sirius withdraw from participation in the Titan project. Then the entire operation underwent revision and change. As the supreme director of all operations, Zeus put the project under more rigid and disciplined management. He did replace all key personnel, and the Titan project did become the Terra experiment. Under Zeus the project became global in scope, as man had migrated from the one area of the Earth to others. Under the direction of Zeus there did take place the "allotments of the gods." The Earth was divided into sectors and new personnel were assigned to duty around the planet. Thus did Poseidon come to oversee the early Atlantean land and people 58,000 years before the appearance of Christ upon the Earth. Zeus did oversee project operations through the remainder of the Lemurian/early Atlantic age, the event of the first cataclysm, and throughout the age of the Atlantic empire.*

*The influence of these and the relations from other star systems of the universe would come to have a great effect upon the people of Atlantis. There was trade and the exchange of ideas and technology. Know that these gods were actual physical beings from technologically advanced civilizations elsewhere in the universe. Ages afterward, mankind, with no recorded history of such events, having only stories borne of misconception and unable to access race memory of their own history, would come to endow these beings with powers and abilities far beyond those of mortal men.*

*Presently, during this fourth cycle of man's progression on Earth, these relations have for the most part restricted themselves from direct involvement and have remained invisible from the eyes of mankind. With the dawn of the twentieth century and increase in the reintroduction of Atlantean tech-*

*nology, the debate among these relations over the concept of direct involvement was renewed. Mankind once again attracts the interest of our space relations. Know that our relatives from the stars are poised and await the great turning of the wheel, which will bring mankind into the fifth cycle, or what you are so fond of referring to as the new age. This will be an age of enlightenment for all mankind and a time of healing for the Earth.*

I had never understood Greek or Roman mythology. Actually, I had always considered the gods to be kind of silly and wondered how anyone could have actually worshiped them. After receiving this information from Tiagorrah, I went to the public library and did a little research into the subject. What I found was quite amazing.

According to earliest Greek myth, it was believed that Uranus and Ge (sky and Earth) "bore" the Titans. According to Tiagorrah, these beings descended from out of the sky to the Earth. There were twelve Titans in all, six male and six female. They were *Oceanos, Coeus, Crieus, Hyperion, Iapetus, Theia, Themis, Rhea, Mnemosyne, Phoebe, Tethys* and *Cronus.* Cronus was the god of the sky, and his sister, Rhea, was the goddess of the Earth. Hyperion drove the sun chariot across the sky each day, while his sister, Selene, drove the moon chariot. Oceanos and Tethys "bore" 3000 sons and 3000 daughters. Cronus and Rhea bore *Hestia, Demeter, Hera, Hades, Poseidon* and *Zeus.*

According to Tiagorrah, Cronos directed project operations from an orbital headquarters. Ree, his assistant and second in authority, was a geologist. *Iperenos, Iyea, Helios* and *Selee* were logistics and transportation personnel. *Oshenos* and *Ethis* represented the study of the oceans and the air. All this alone required a work force of 6000 personnel.

In classical mythology the first divine rulers of the Earth were the Titans. Cronus, with his brothers and sisters, ruled over the Earth for thousands of years during a golden age among men. Then Cronus learned from Ge and Uranus that he would come to be overthrown by his own child. Fearing this, he swallowed each one as it came forth from its mother so that no other descendant of Uranus would obtain kingly power. Grief took hold of Rhea when she was about to bring forth Zeus. She entreated her parents to help her bring forth her child in secret and allow Uranus and the eaten children to exact revenge. Rhea went in secret to bear Zeus and Ge received him from her. When Zeus had grown to maturity, Cronus was beguiled by Rhea to bring up all that he had swallowed.

Zeus, with his disgorged brothers and sisters as allies, waged war against his father, Cronus, and the other Titans. The two sides came together with a great clamor, attacking each other in a mighty battle. Then Zeus came thundering down from the heavens, hurling bolts of lightning and holy flame. The hot blasts engulfed the Titans and they were defeated. Cronus was deposed by Zeus and retired to a distant realm known as the Island of the Blessed.

Zeus was established as king of the gods. He assumed the sky as his realm and initiated the "allotments of the gods." His brothers and sisters shared in divine power over the Earth, and each served various functions. Zeus mated with goddesses and mortal women, and his offspring who were also gods and goddesses, were given various powers and abilities as they were born. They were *Hebe, Aries, Hephaestus, Apollo, Artemus, Dionysis, Athena, Hermes* and *Aphrodite.*

According to Plato's account of the Atlantis legend, the Egyptian archivists and priests spoke of the "allotments of the gods," and that the gods "did distribute the whole of the Earth into portions of differing extent." These were assigned among the gods for each to rule. This is how Poseidon came to rule over Atlantis.

*Know that the allotments of the gods is in reference to the planetary survey maps and charts, which divided the landmasses of the planet into var-*

*ious sectors for the purpose of reference, navigation and study. There were many such maps, those as pertained to the geology, atmosphere and electromagnetism — this similar to present transmissions from your spacecrafts and satellites. Such maps and photographs were common among our visiting relations from the stars. Several of these were presented to various government officials and to several temples in Poseidon.*

The account of Hesiod, writing in the seventh century B.C., is the earliest account that has survived to this day. The similarities between Tiagorrah's information and mythology are striking. The more I thought about it, the more questions I had. Were the gods of ancient Greece, who lived atop the mountain of Olympus, actually kings and queens of Atlantis? Was Atlantis Olympus? If you examine Greek mythology, can you piece together bits of Atlantean history? Tiagorrah, always quite aware of my thoughts and wonderings, responded in his usual way.

*The power struggle between elements of our relations from the stars is the foundation of the Greek myths concerning war between the gods and the Titans — this from the event of a great confrontation on the surface of the Earth, to the time when Cronus and his supporters retreated to the sanctuary of the Mars transfer base. Zeus and his people did eventually defeat them there, thus ending that decade of dispute.*

*The rule of Zeus and the Terra experiment brought about what has been described as a golden age for Atlantis. Poseidon did become the first king of Atlantis and brought great change to our people. Atlas became the second king, as he did succeed his father, Poseidon. He was an omnipotent ruler of Atlantis, which was very powerful at that time, and held great influence throughout the Earth. Thus Atlas is depicted in myth as a great giant, holding the Earth upon his shoulders.*

*To know the history of Atlantis is to understand mythology. The gods and goddesses of Greece were those of our relations from the stars, who did influence the Atlantean people long ago. Their descendants were the royal lineage, who did successively rule Atlantis during the latter period of the Lemurian/early Atlantic age.*

*Though our relations did monitor geologic activities and conditions, the actual event of the first cataclysm caught them unaware and caused great disruption to their operations. During the next age, that of the Atlantic empire, their influence on Atlantean government decreased considerably, whereas trade and technological assistance increased. With the event of the second cataclysm, these relations did reevaluate their involvement.*

*Early into the late Atlantic age, our relations from the stars did adopt strict laws of noninterference and did end their association with mankind. During the late Atlantic age, Atlantis, though still a great power, never regained the technology, wealth or splendor of her past.*

*Know that the third and final cataclysm which befell Atlantis took place nearly 12,000 years ago from present. Know that this day there exist and are known to you ancient Egyptian scrolls which refer to the reign of the gods over Egypt thousands of years before the first recorded dynasty. This relates to the influence of Atlantis over the Egyptian lands during the late Atlantic age.*

The more I read about Greek mythology and compared it to Tiagorrah's information, the more all the myths about gods and goddesses seemed to make sense. I was looking at it all from a different perspective — that of Tiagorrah.

# Star Relations in Egypt

*Into orbit above the land which this day is known as Egypt, there came to be Ra. After traveling a vast distance, his great ship did enter the Earth's atmosphere. It did descend from the sky and come to rest upon the Earth. Its flight did resemble that of the current space shuttles, for there was great fire and sound. Thus did Ra make his arrival upon this world. In this present age there may be difficulty in conceptualizing such an occurrence so distant past. To present understanding, Ra was the Egyptian god of the sun and lord of the sky, a religious deity of an ancient people long gone. Know that Ra came to this Earth as part of the Titan project. Such did take place during the Lemurian age.*

*Ra was of our relations from the star system of Orion. These worked in conjunction with their Pleiadian, Sirian and Arcturan relations as an integral part of the overall program. Their field of study was the animal kingdom. Their purpose was to catalog and classify the vast multitude of species, to observe and understand animal evolution, intelligence and behavior. The land which is now Egypt was chosen as a center of operations for that purpose, in an area of the Earth which was abundant with new Life then. This included a very sparse population of early men. These had migrated to the area from Lemuria and early Atlantis, the latter having come up through the African land. Ra would come to have great influence over these early inhabitants.*

*Ra brought forth Shoo and Tefnoot. Know that Shu was the Orion linguistic equivalent of what you would term* shuttle *and that Tefnut was the equivalent of* transport. *Define Geb as Earth G, or ground, and Nut (newt) as sky, or orbital. Ra, in other words, set up shuttle transportation between the orbital spacecraft and the planet surface.*

*Ra did institute the direct-contact project. Such could be defined as research which involved direct influence and manipulation of that which was the subject of study. Procedures freely utilized in regard to animal research were applied to mankind. Ra was a supporter of those Pleiadian elements which pro-*

*posed that the Titan project expand to include the Atlantean civilization. He was a great influence upon Zeus and Poseidon, who did later install their own form of direct contact program in the Atlantean land. Soon after Cronos surrendered the Titan project to Zeus did Ra turn over control of Orion operations to Thoth. Then Ra departed the Earth to monitor involvement from an orbital control center. There would be many to hold the position of Ra.*

*Thoth was a highly evolved being who would be born into the physical Earth experience three times. When Thoth was given authority from Ra, he took on the form of man for the first time. He went to the Egyptian land, and from that perspective Thoth did observe, oversee and record the experience. Upon completion, Thoth did turn over the project to Osiris.*

*The project was modified by Osiris in order to promote agriculture and civilization. He attempted to raise his subjects' level of knowledge and understanding. Thus the Orion direct-contact experiment progressed to a new level. There were those who opposed Osiris and his program. This was, after all, a departure from the Orion focus of mission as related to the overall Titan project. Seth, chief zoologist at the time, did organize opposition against him and did induce the Titan group to suspend Osiris. Horus, second to Osiris and slated to be his successor, struck out in defense of Osiris and against Seth.*

*Confrontation took place between these elements.*

*Isis, mate of Osiris, and her supporters did convince the Titan group authorities to reinstate Osiris and continue project operations. There followed a full investigation, assessment and evaluation of Osiris and his project. There was open debate amidst the Titan Council of Directors on Mars base, as both sides did argue their positions. It came to be that Osiris did turn over authority to Horus, and the project would have continued had not the first great cataclysm then taken place. This disrupted all operations. The program did suddenly go off line, so to speak. After the event it was resumed under Horus, and our relations did then aid and assist mankind during the difficult time of healing and reconstruction.*

*Horus did turn over authority to Thoth, who had manifested himself as an Atlantean at that time, this being his second Earth experience in human form. Therefore he did continue the project from that perspective. Under Thoth, there were great leaps of progress and growth in Egypt in all areas of mankind's endeavors, for he did promote the Atlantean influence there. But the Atlantean empire would prove corrupt and arrogant. It would threaten harmonious coexistence and cause war and destruction.*

*Thoth had a knowing of the turning of the wheels*

*and could see ahead what the Atlantean empire would bring. Therefore Thoth did withdraw himself from the experience and was the last of his kind—this as Amillius became the first emperor and the Atlantean empire was born.*

The Egyptian creation story is very similar to that of the early Greeks. In Egyptian beliefs, Nun was believed to be the primordial waters from which everything came into being. This is much the same as Chaos meant to the Greeks. Atom was seen by Egyptians as the creative force, which manifested itself as Ra. (In Greek myth Eros was the creative force.) Ra was the god of the sun and lord of the skies. He ruled over the first universe, known to the Egyptians as the first world. During this first world men and gods lived together upon the Earth. Ra would get into his sacred ship each day, travel across the sky and inspect the twelve provinces of his kingdom.

According to Egyptian mythology, Ra, the sun god, brought forth Shu and Tefnut. Shu (shoo) was the air, or "he who holds things up." Tefnut (teff-noot) was the clouds, or "she who helps hold things up." Shu and Tefnut brought forth Geb (jeb) and Nut (noot). Geb was the Earth and Nut, the sky. In ancient depictions Geb is represented by a reclining male figure, upon whose body exist all things. Nut is represented as the sky. Her figure arches over the reclining Geb, and upon her body are the stars. According to myth, Geb and Nut came together in sexual union. Shu was ordered by Ra to separate the two, but by then it was too late. Geb and Nut brought forth gods and goddesses. In other words, beings from the sky came to Earth and mingled with the inhabitants.

As time passed and Ra slowly got old, men began to plot against him. So Ra sent his eye, which had a mind of its own, to rush upon them and massacre them. Eventually, the ingratitude of mankind made Ra distasteful of the world. Desiring to withdraw, he abdicated his position to Thoth. Then Nut bore Ra upon her back to the heavens. Ra then circled the Earth each day in his boat of a million years. He was the first of "seven divine rulers" of Egypt. It is written that "the forms of Ra were as many as seventy-five."

According to Egyptian mythology, there were seven gods who would ultimately hold the position of divine ruler over the Egyptian land. Ra was the first, Thoth was the second. Then there was Shu, Geb, Osiris, Horus and then Thoth again. Shu and Geb were considered by the ancient Egyptians as actual god-beings who ruled over Egypt.

*The Shu-Geb rulership may be taken to refer to first contacts with early shuttle pilots and support personnel. Once regular service was established, Geb, or ground base, was the center of Orion operations in that part of the world. Understand the Shu-Geb rulership as a reference to the control of Egypt from orbital headquarters (Shu) and the control of operations from ground base (Geb).*

In Egyptian mythology, Osiris was the fifth divine ruler of Egypt. He introduced certain tools and taught his subjects agriculture and law. Therefore, Osiris came to be known as "the good one." Osiris and Isis ruled as king and queen together, and bore Horus. Later on Osiris was plotted against by his brother, Seth. When Osiris was killed by conspirators, Horus set out to avenge his father, which culminated in war.

Meanwhile, Isis had undertaken a "great journey" to recover the body of Osiris. Aided by Thoth and Anubis, she managed to restore Life to Osiris. The war between Horus and Seth was then terminated in a draw. Before the tribunal of the gods, Osiris answered Seth's accusations. The result was that Osiris chose to depart from the Earth and return to the Elysian fields.

Horus was declared Divine Ruler over Upper and Lower Egypt. He was the sixth. Later on, when Horus left earthly power, he was succeeded by Thoth. Thoth ruled over the Egyptian land for 3226 years. He was the keeper of the divine archives and endowed with great knowledge and wisdom. Thoth was the inventor of hieroglyphics, the calendar, arithmetic, magic, music and medicine. After his long reign on Earth, Thoth ascended into the sky to dwell in the heavens. He was the last of the divine rulers.

The Egyptian creation story, its mythology and symbolism of the origins of the gods, is similar to that of the early Greeks. Ge and Uranus begat Cronus; Shu and Tefnut begat Ra. In both cases the Earth and the sky produced the sun god. There were periods during which the gods ruled over the Earth. In the Egyptian story, Ra was the first of seven divine rulers. In the Greek myth, first there were the twelve Titans, then there was Zeus and the gods. Much of both Egyptian and Greek mythology corresponds to events described by Tiagorrah. The many similarities complement each other, and what comes together is a fascinating scenario.

I put the creation stories and the mythical origins of the gods into a simplified listing of three categories. These consist of the Egyptian, the Greek, then Tiagorrah's versions. Comparing the three, I found that they all fit together rather nicely — Nun, Chaos and the void; Atom, Eros and creation; and Geb and Nut, Uranus and Ge, Earth and sky. The three creation stories seem to have a lot in common, shown in the following chart.

| EGYPTIAN | GREEK | TIAGORRAH |
| --- | --- | --- |
| Nun | Chaos | Void |
| Atom | Eros | Creation |
| Geb and Nut | Uranus and Ge | Earth and sky |
| Ra | Titans | Lemuria |
| gods rule | gods rule | Early Atlantic |
| gods rule | gods rule | Atlantic empire |
| End of the gods' rule on Earth | | Late Atlantic |
| Tales of the gods | | Modern age |

Ra and the Titans ruled over the Earth from the beginning of the Lemurian/early Atlantic age. The reign of the divine rulers of Egypt and that of Zeus and the gods over the Earth began during the early Atlantic age and continues into the time of the Atlantean empire. After the destruction of the empire, the gods reevaluated their association with mankind. Early into the late Atlantic age they ended their association with mankind. Finally, during this modern age we have only ancient mythology and the tales of the gods, with their limited perspectives on lost histories. To most, the gods and their stories are merely so much silly nonsense. But then, as Tiagorrah would say, our own perspectives are very limited because of our limited perception.

Tiagorrah has said that Atlantis had an influence in Egypt since before Poseidon, and that Atlantean involvement there continued right up to the third cataclysm, which occurred around 10,000 B.C. He stated that the construction of the Sphinx complex was first begun by Atlantean descendants over 15,000 years ago. At the time the Sphinx was constructed, the climate was different from that of today. There were trees and vegetation and an abundance of wildlife.

The temple located beside the Sphinx was constructed of great stone blocks which had been quarried from around the body of the Sphinx, creating the Sphinx's present enclosure. This temple is of Atlantean influence. It was built by descendants of Atlantis who populated the area at that time. This would have been during the closing centuries of the late Atlantic age. All this points to an advanced civilization preceding that of the Egyptians, the roots of which were Atlantean.

## Order of Events
## 80,000 B.C. through 5000 B.C.

| | |
|---|---|
| **80,000 B.C.** | perfected vehicle in Lemuria |
| **70,000 B.C.** | perfected vehicle in Atlantia |
| | Atlantia founded |
| | Temple of One in Atlantia |
| | Ra in Egypt |
| | Zeus replaces Cronos |
| **58,000 B.C.** | space relations to Atlantis |
| | Poseidon as overseer |

| | |
|---|---|
| | Thoth replaces Ra |
| | Temple of the Sun |
| | construction of the Atlantia rings |
| | Poseidon as king |
| | city is named Poseidon |
| | royal lineage of kings and queens |
| | Belial as king |
| | Sons of Belial |
| **48,000 B.C.** | Event of the first great cataclysm destroying Lemuria |
| | healing |
| | reconstruction |
| | government transition |
| **41,500 B.C.** | birth of the empire |
| **28,000 B.C.** | second cataclysm |
| **13,000 B.C.** | Sphinx construction began |
| **12,000 B.C.** | Temple of Sphinx constructed |
| **10,000 B.C.** | third cataclysm |
| **5,000 B.C.** | beginning of recorded history |

# Descriptions of Early Atlantis

*Know that over 70,000 years ago from present, Lemurian explorers did travel to, and settle upon, the land which later came to be known as Atlantis. The first man to circumnavigate the continent was Ammus, who described it as "a massive island, larger than our own, centered within the vast ocean to the east."*

*I would provide descriptions of early Atlantis. I would speak as concerns the period before the arrival of Poseidon. Know that over 65,000 years ago, early Atlanteans did live within tribal units, similar in many ways to the tribal peoples of present experience. There were four primary tribal groups, each of these composed of a number of lesser sub-*

*groups. Our people did live in peace within a natural environment of abundance. This is not to imply that there was no conflict or confrontation, but that all lived under the Law of One then, and so were in harmony with the flow of the continuum, the natural flow of Life.*

*Living in harmony with the Life force under the Law of One, mankind had not begun to fully develop the capacity for the emotion of anger. This negative has developed over time with the loss of the truth of the One Law from the knowledge of mankind. The experience of this emotion was not an unknown to our people, but anger was generally considered undignified and contrary to the One Law. Its occurrence was considered an unusual display of negative energy and was rare by modern standards. This emotion is commonplace in the present society, as is violence, rage and the capacity for hatred. Thus can flourish intolerance and conflict in the individual sense or in the collective form of war.*

*According to the Law of One, all Life is sacred, and so it followed that in the event of conflict, the intent of the combatants was not to inflict death or injury to the physical being, but to prevail over an adversary in a symbolic manner, to cause insult to one's opponent rather than injury — this similar to the concept of sport or much the same as the Native*

*American tradition of counting coups.*

*Under the Law of One, council government did flourish. Everyone had a voice in the affairs of the community, for all did actively participate in the collective, and no voice was unimportant. Council government was all-inclusive. Lesser councils comprised larger councils, which culminated in that of the Great Council. This was the wheels within the wheels of our people's cooperative union under the One Law.*

*I would describe this early period as the Golden Age of Atlantis, for all lived in harmony under the Law of One before the event of the arrival of outside forces and the introduction and development of negative thoughts and emotions.*

*These early Atlanteans were aware of the existence of a truly sacred place, a healing site for the mind and body, for the heart and soul. This was a special site, one of energy and power. Such would be termed this day a vortex of Earth energies. This is where the four tribes came together, as it was considered to be common ground, sacred land, the center of our circle. Here came to be the Great Circle, the symbol of the One Law and the place where all people came together. Here did meet the Great Council and take place the annual gatherings. There would come to be a temple erected there, the Temple of One.*

*There evolved that the people would live on the lands around and beyond this sacred site. They did not construct their dwellings on the site itself, for it was not considered proper to live on sacred ground. This was a place of ceremony, sacred land for the purpose of communion with the Creator and with nature. The people of all tribes did share a common temple and holy place there. The earlier Lemurian settlers and priests had called this place Atlantia, for in their language "atlante" meant "that land." And so the people collectively came to be known as the people of Atlantia, or Atlanteans.*

*Upon the vast island continent there were great mountains and there were also volcanic peaks. There were, as well, lands of various elevations, and beyond these the great open plain. Many who did cultivate, and those who were agriculturalists, were highly honored for their knowledge and ability to harmoniously interact with and utilize the natural Earth energies. Under the One Law, the sacred gift of the Creator must be honored; Earth must be acknowledged for all she provides. Thus these growers were also priests as well. The proper prayers, rituals and ceremonials had to be performed in order for the end products to be acceptable, not only for the people but for Creator.*

*Since things of a spiritual nature were a part of everyday Life, then everyday activities had a spiritu-*

*al logic as well. For example, to eat was a spiritual act, for one must nourish the physical vehicle, which is sacred. Therefore, one must perform ritual prayer and give thanks to Creator. One must also acknowledge the physical source of that which is consumed. To Atlanteans of the time, such things as these were understood and acknowledged routinely.*

*Another example would be that giving was a part of Life to our people. As the Creator gives freely to all people, so all people should give freely of themselves. Such is the Law of One, and so the more an individual did give to others, then it followed that this individual would be honored by others. This was not always giving in the material sense, but a giving of the self out of the generosity of the heart. Under the Law of One, all are related, all are One, and so we did conduct ourselves then.*

*If that which I have related appears as though a description of the Native American culture of your present experience, it is due to the fact that Native American culture has best preserved a knowledge of One Law principles through the passage of time — this after receiving same from Atlantean contact many ages past.*

According to Tiagorrah, the Native Americans (and other tribal peoples worldwide) have best preserved the Law of One through the ages. Through my own association with Indian traditions and culture, having been a traditional northern-style dancer participating in Native American ceremonies, I must agree with Tiagorrah's assertion.

> There is natural power, and there is spiritual power. In the old days, my people did not separate daily life in the world from spiritual life. Everything was spiritual, our attitude was spiritual, and *Wakan Tanka* was involved in everything we said and did.
>
> — Fools Crow, Teton Sioux, 1975

> All things are connected. Whatever befalls the Earth befalls the sons of the Earth. Man did not weave the web of Life, he is only a strand in it. Whatever he does to the web, he does to himself.
>
> — Chief Seattle, Nez Perce, 1854

Are these the words of an ignorant, uncivilized people, or do these sound more like the words of One Law priests? Tiagorrah continues:

*From her shores, the continent of Atlantis was not far distant from the lands known this day as the Americas, Africa and Europe. The early Atlanteans did carry on exploration and trade in those parts of the world. They did also carry on trade with Lemuria, then dominant in the Earth. This early intercontinental travel could be described as a trickle in comparison to the amount of trade and expansionism that would follow in the age of the empire. Early on, however, such contact and trade did involve the appearance of small outposts and colonies upon the far continents. The outpost, or trading post, was the nucleus for most of these early colonies. The trickles did expand with the progression of related technology, the arrival of our cosmic relations, the conception and growth of the city of Poseidon and the reign of the royal lineage of kings and queens before the event of the first cataclysm. By the time of that event, Atlantis had established herself in many areas of the Earth.*

*I would speak at this time concerning the city of Poseidon. I would describe that city and those persons who did contribute to the history of that land, the site which was the sacred ground known as Atlantia and upon which did develop the greatest city ever to exist upon the Earth.*

*It was early in the history of Atlantis and her people when our relatives from the stars did make their presence known to us. We did refer to them as our relations, for so they are under the Law of One. These did consider the people of Atlantis to be advanced beings with great technological capabilities. They did initiate physical contact, out of which there developed communications and exchange.*

*At first, the purpose of our space relations had been to study and observe the evolution and devel-*

*opment of the human race on Earth. This had been the Titan's purpose of mission. Under Zeus, our relations did undertake the study of mankind in order to determine the true nature of same through a program which involved the introduction of certain information, material and technology, thus to observe over the course of time the manner in which mankind utilized the resources. Ultimately, they sought to determine if mankind would come to join in the cosmic circle, so to speak, or if mankind would prove to be of an aggressive nature. So did the focus of these relations shift at that time. So did Zeus authorize, and Poseidon initiate, their direct-contact experiment, which was the Terran Project.*

*The person in command of all planetary operations was the one who did come to be known as Zeus, the overlord of his people — this not as the name of an individual but as a certain level of leadership, the rank of an officer. The individual who did maintain authority over all operations and personnel within the Atlantis sector was the sector leader, who was Poseidon. He had been assigned to that position by order of Zeus.*

*It was Poseidon who did address the High Council of Elders and convince that body to support trade and exchange programs between our peoples. Poseidon did acknowledge many aspects of the One Law, which did impress the Council and help sway their decision.*

*Poseidon would come to have great influence over the Atlantean land. His official mission was to oversee research and exchange programs, the observation and evaluation of the progress of these programs, and the effects of same upon the Atlantic people and their culture. Poseidon would come to indulge himself therein. It was the intent of Poseidon to carry his mission to the very limits of his authority, to go so far as to tamper with the leadership and government of Atlantis. Poseidon did set Atlantis on a road of great development and progress, his motivation being to ensure his own greatness in Atlantic history. It would be his will to install his own bloodline into leadership over Atlantis.*

*It happened that during a tour of the land which was Atlantia, Poseidon was introduced to the priestess Cleiteah. She was in residence at the One Temple with those few charged as stewards of the land. This meeting would come to have great consequence for Atlantis, for Poseidon would take the priestess Cleiteah to be his wife. Together, Poseidon and Cleiteah did spend many hours at the temple complex within the land of Atlantia. It was the will of Poseidon to have there prepared private quarters for himself and his wife. So it came to be that Poseidon, also known as the Great Manipulator, did all this and more.*

*His influence over Atlantis and her people did grow, as he promised magnificent temples for religion, education and medicine. He promised opulent facilities for government and law, great centers for research and for the arts, industrial and economic growth and improvement—all this and more for Atlantis and her people.*

*Poseidon proposed that a great wall, plated in bright copper, be constructed along the perimeter of Atlantia. It would symbolize the sacred circle of the One Law, a sacred symbol throughout the universe. Poseidon did thus conspire, and so it did come to be, that the land of Atlantia was encircled with a great wall, and around this was constructed a circular harbor.*

*At the event of the project's completion ceremony, Poseidon did address the Atlantean people and congratulate them on their accomplishment. He proudly proclaimed that it was a magnificent monument to the One Law and proof of the ingenuity and ability of mankind for unlimited possibilities of the future. The great circle was visible from orbiting spacecraft. Poseidon did present several high-altitude photographs of the completed project to high-ranking Atlantean officials, myself included.*

*Poseidon would go on to have encircled the lands which lay outside of the Atlantia ring, the lands where the people did have their dwelling places—*

*this again with wall and with harbor. Poseidon would also come to have encircled vast areas of land beyond these. So did the form of that great city evolve. The city did grow and prosper through the centuries to become the most magnificent city ever to exist upon the Earth. It became the capital city of the great Atlantean empire, and it survived two great cataclysms.*

*The sacred center of the city contained the religious, educational and government facilities. The secondary ring of land was reserved for the general population. The third ring of land was for the purpose of agriculture, industry and trade. Harbors were connected by a central canal to the vast ocean.*

*Poseidon, the Great Manipulator, did overstep the limits of his authority in many of his actions. His involvement with the priestess Cleiteah did come to have great consequence for Atlantis, for together Poseidon and Cleiteah introduced five pair of offspring. Of these, Atlas was the senior male.*

*As time did pass, the ten matured. Through the political manipulations of Poseidon, Atlantis was apportioned out among the ten. They ruled their lands through a council government over which Atlas did preside. The descendants of these ruled in succession thereafter, until the time of the Earth shift which brought destruction to Lemuria and great change to Atlantis.*

*Atlas did maintain the strength of leadership over matters of state, as exhibited by his father before him. It was Atlas who did oversee the completion of the great Temple of Poseidon in Atlantia. He did cause to be constructed a beautiful palace residence for himself and grand facilities for government. All of this would be further embellished by the succession of rulers to follow.*

*Atlas wed Pleioneh, the daughter of Oshenos, great mariner and builder of ships. Together, Atlas and Pleioneh produced seven daughters. These would come to be known as the Pleiades, named for the seven Pleiadian stars. These seven would eventually be transported to their ancestral home world for their educational development.*

*Much later on in time, after the demise of the empire, Zeus did gather advisors from among his people. They did reevaluate their involvement with mankind—this due to the degeneration of man's spirituality, ideals and morality. There did come the time when Zeus and his people did terminate their involvement with mankind. They adopted strict laws of noninterference and there was no more intercommunication or exchange. They no longer allowed confirmation of their existence by the human inhabitants of the planet Terra. In recent years some of our space relations have reevaluated their positions concerning this policy and have modified certain aspects of same due to more recent developments.*

*There were many visitors to the planet Terra in those ages past. Know you now the foundation of those legends and myths which developed through time around Poseidon and that great city.*

*In describing aspects of early Atlantean history, it is important that I speak concerning Belial to provide an understanding of the nature of that being. Know that Belial was brother to Atlan. These were sons of a powerful king who reigned over 2000 years before the event of the first cataclysm, during the time of the powerful rulers of the old order.*

*Atlan held great interest in studies at the Temple of One and did excel in religion and sociology. Atlan, due to his royal lineage and position as a prince of the realm, did spend many hours engaged in conversation with many high-ranking government officials as well as the great thinkers and philosophers of the day. He came to be held in high esteem by many great Atlanteans of the time.*

*Belial, also of royal lineage and position, was as highly intelligent and educated as was his brother Atlan. He did excel in all areas of endeavor. Belial did, however, have a dark side to his nature. He did hold resentment and jealousy toward his brother. As the eldest, Atlan would inherit all authority and power from his father, the king. Belial would, there-*

*fore, consistently uphold an opposing viewpoint to that of Atlan. He did reject the teachings of the One Law.*

*Belial believed in intellect and technology, power and manipulation like his hero, Poseidon. He believed that mankind, having gained intellect, creativity and free will, rightly inherits dominion over the Earth and its destiny. He cited the Atlantean civilization in example, having been brought about through man's own collective manifestation. Atlantis herself was proof of this.*

*Belial believed that man's collective will to progress and evolve would continually expand and accelerate. He believed that the Creator had intended unlimited prosperity for Atlantis and her people. Belial's views would come to influence many people. He did become very popular and very powerful.*

*Thus began a new movement among the people, a movement which would become a religious and political force. It would be a religion which stood for progress and unlimited prosperity. It would be a political force which stood for military power and Atlantean expansionism.*

*It would come to be that Belial did force his brother Atlan from power. Belial did then rule that province of Atlantis which was the greatest and most powerful, that province wherein lay the capital, which was Poseidon. He did will to thrust Atlantis into a period of record growth and prosperity no matter what means were employed to achieve the desired results. He did bring about what you would term the original secret society, that which was the Sons of Belial, through which his philosophy would be handed down and his ultimate goal perpetuated to realization. Belial envisioned Atlantis as a truly global empire which would ultimately expand into space. Belial did believe that Atlantean technology would one day carry the empire to include other worlds. I shall impart some of the famous words of Belial.*

> Those of the Pleiades, Orion, Sirius and others may appear to be superior beings, and they may appear to command superior technology, but there will come a day when they shall see that we of Atlantis are the master race!
>
> We are, in ourselves, gods! Not only through our royal lineage, but through our own intelligence and device. When all work together toward the one goal, then no achievement is too great and no obstacle insurmountable. Not today or tomorrow, but in ages to come the arms of the Atlantean empire shall reach out to the stars!
>
> — Belial, King of Poseidia

*These things did take place early in the history of Atlantis, when Lemuria still held great influence in the Earth. Later on in time, Belial would be remembered as "the father of the Empire." The Sons of Belial were a political and religious power associated with the Temple of the Sun. In the era of the empire these forces did rule. They would bring great cataclysm and destruction such that would change the face of the Earth.*

# The Order of the Word

*Greetings. I would speak as concerns early Atlantean ventures to the far lands of the Earth. Know that very early in Atlantean history there were those who did undertake the challenges of long-distance travel. Such long journeys were of many years duration. Those returned from such travel carried with them great wealth of knowledge; others did never return to the mother island.*

*There were priests of the One Law who did journey to far lands in order to explore, to gain knowledge of the Earth and other Life forms, to learn from any peoples they might encounter, and to offer the teachings and meaning of the circle as did relate to the Law of One. This was the Order of the Word, which did go out from the Temple of One in this capacity. And so the priests of the Order of the Word were explorers, naturalists and information gatherers as well as teachers. They found peoples who had formed circles out of earlier Lemurian contact. They did also find others with no knowledge of same.*

*The Spirit by which these priests did conduct themselves was different by far from that which drove the explorers of the fifteenth and sixteenth centuries which are familiar to you. Atlantean priests did study all things natural, and they sought understanding of the peoples they encountered. Their quest was for the obtainment of knowledge as well as the dissemination of same. Those peoples who exhibited an eagerness to learn would receive information. In return they would share of their own knowledge. In this way did the Law of One spread through the far lands in the early times of Atlantean history.*

*When Poseidon and his people came upon Atlantis, the Order of the Word and its activities did expand, for there were those who would not accept the changes which Poseidon initiated. At this point in time, Poseidon's every word was popular among the majority of the Atlantean people. The High Council and most of the general public did support Poseidon's proposals, for it was considered to be the dawn of a new age. Thus was viewed the arrival of our relations from the stars. Their ideas and technology did compel the Atlantean people to accept much and to question little. Perhaps many of them, in their naiveté, were like children, yet there were those who questioned, as it should be.*

*The Order of the Word was supported by the Pleiadians, the temple leaders and the participating priests and priestesses, though each element did so out of differing motivations. The temple leaders expanded the program to placate the dissenters; the Pleiadians, to eliminate them from the Atlantis theater. Those active within the Order itself were there primarily due to the fact that they opposed Pleiadian influence over the Atlantia issue. They saw the alteration of Atlantia as a desecration of that land. Through the Order they did seek out other places of power and form new circles elsewhere in the world. With the reign of the descendants of Poseidon, others would seek to separate themselves from the "progress" of Atlantean civilization.*

*By the event of the first cataclysm, Atlantis was firmly established in many areas of the Earth. This did include the Americas, Europe and Africa. There was the settlement in the region you know as the Four Corners area of the American Southwest. Here both Lemuria and Atlantis shared involvement. The Hopi tribe retains akashic memory of this "first world." Tibetans, Hindus, Native Americans and various other tribal peoples have retained ancient soul memories through the roots of their spiritual practices and beliefs.*

*The most ancient of all religious symbols, the circle, dates back to the Lemurian/early Atlantic age. The fire, as the heart and center of the circle; as the transmuter of energy; as that into which are placed prayers and offerings; as the beacon which draws in the spiritual elements — has been so since that long-ago age.*

*Mankind has now drifted far from his understanding of the One Law, labeling those who still incorporate some basic One Law knowledge and practice in their belief system as being paganistic and primitive.*

# The Atlantean Ritual of Awakening

*Greetings. I would speak as concerns a form of learning which Atlanteans did practice long ago. This was the ritual of awakening, the rite of understanding that which was known as the nature-walk experience. It was one of passage into adulthood, an important step in the transition of youth into responsible and enlightened adults. All youth of Atlantis did undergo this ritual, from the early period before Poseidon until the event of the first cataclysm. Later, very early in the era of the Atlantic empire, it was revived by One Law priests and did continue through that period.*

*The people of those times past did communicate telepathically with each other and all other Life forms. The nature walk did play an important role in furthering the development of telepathic ability as well as, more importantly, One Law understanding. It did enhance one's connection to Earth's energies, to the natural order of all creation and to One Law reality. It did clarify the perception and promote insight, strengthen one spiritually and raise One Law consciousness. Through this experience did the youth learn, progress and evolve. Such was the purpose of this important ceremony. Later, throughout their long lifetimes, they might choose to undertake the nature walk many times, for it was also a ritual of meditation, healing, renewal and empowerment.*

*All youth between the ages of sixteen to twenty years did participate in this ritual of awakening. An educator-priest did determine when a youth had grown and developed to the extent that he be eligible for this important undertaking. It was the educator who did determine the duration of ritual, which could be up to seven days in length. He did also choose the area of placement, which was always a secluded natural environment. This could be along the vast coastal area or far inland, beside a valley stream or atop a great mountain. Wherever the location, it was important that the participant be alone, away from human contact and any disturbances or distractions which could be incurred by same.*

*When a youth was ready to undergo the nature walk, the educator did take that person to the chosen site, around which he was instructed to mark out a large circle, using natural materials. This was usually fifty-six yards in diameter, and within which the youth was left alone for the determined length of time. In the middle of this great circle he did then prepare his personal ceremonial prayer circle. This did extend seven feet from a central fire pit. When not engaged in prayer or meditation, he was free to enter or exit the prayer circle at any time but was forbidden to cross over the outer perimeter of the placement area. The youth was restricted from the intake of nourishment during the ritual and was permitted to drink only water. This did increase awareness, attune the perception and aid in the elevation of telepathic ability.*

*And so the youth did stay alone within the placement area for the determined length of time in order to commune with his inner self and all of creation. He was able to tune into, and communicate with, the beings and Spirits, the elements and energies, all Life forms around him, all of nature. All these possess knowledge, and from them the youth did learn about Life, Love, Earth and Spirit. They did speak to him about the Law of One and taught him about his relationship to the Earth and all living things.*

*At the end of the ritual time span, the educator*

*did appear to the youth, and together they returned to the temple. There the youth was cleansed and did eat and sleep. After he had rested, he did have counsel with his educator concerning the experience.*

*Temples were more than places of spirituality and religion; they were also centers for research and education. In residence were educators, researchers, scientists, engineers and artists. Temples were vast pools of knowledge and understanding, of creativity and the arts. A youth could receive education within several temples and build several careers during his long lifetime.*

*The seven-day ritual was practiced by those who were inclined toward a road of religion and spirituality, in that seven was considered a sacred number related to the higher chakral frequencies. The greater number of youth were inclined toward other areas of interest and experience. Most did spend a period of four days in nature walk, in that four was considered a sacred number in connection with the Earth, with the physical and natural plane and with the vibrational frequencies of the lower chakras.*

*At times there were those youth who did seek to alter the experience in order to control or predominate over same. Thus they did attempt to manipulate conditions so as to accomplish mastery over the natural environment. It was these who derived little benefit from their nature-walk experience, as they chose not to learn but to control instead.*

*In those ages past, Atlanteans did utilize their natural telepathic abilities and could easily communicate without the use of spoken words. Thus they were able to communicate with and learn from all Life forms. Through telepathic communication one did form a connection with the other. With this state of connection did come understanding and acknowledgment of universal truths, that humanity is a part of the whole, the All That Is, that all of creation is interconnected, that all is One. It is the experience of this oneness that brings understanding of the One Law.*

*The Atlantean people did develop their telepathic abilities throughout their lifetimes. Know that these people of long ago did experience a great longevity of life. As you can comprehend seventy, eighty or ninety years in your experience, try to imagine seven, eight or nine hundred years in physical being. Life expectancy then was over a thousand years. In the physical environment of less molecular density, biologic degeneration took place at a rate less than one-tenth that of present experience. Physical growth, however, did take place at a rate very similar to that which occurs presently, that of your own experience and understanding. Thus it was that with such a long life span, there was ample time for telepathic abilities to be fully developed.*

*I would ask that you consider the nature of the teachings which are imparted to the youth of this day. Do these young people gain a true knowledge and understanding of Life and the world around them? Do they learn of their connection and responsibility to the Earth, to one another and all other Life forms? Do they learn to honor, respect and give thanks for all of creation and all that Creator has provided? Or do they learn to have interests in other, less healthful areas?*

*Education this day has become too focused on job preparation, and the advancement of the individual in this materialistic, consumer-oriented society. The true values of Life, and that which relates to same, have virtually been lost to the present-day education system.*

*Youth need to learn that which pertains to Life, Love, Earth and Spirit, the four points of the Atlantean "medicine wheel," the four points of the circle, which represents the Law of One. Teach them relationship not only to each other, but to all that share Life, the great gift of the Creator. Teach them of procreation and parenthood. Teach them that we are the caretakers of our Mother Earth. Teach them that Love is the most powerful force in the universe, and that they should always carry Love in their hearts to share with others wherever they go. These are the things which were taught to us by all our relations during that long-ago age. I have no more to impart on this subject at present.*

# The Earth Keepers

*In the early times, under the Law of One the Earth and all Life forms were held to be sacred. It was not for man to alter the Creator's design; it was for man to live in harmony within the context of creation. Alteration of place could be undertaken only after careful consideration of the spiritual aspects and implications of same. The resultant physical impact upon all elements directly affected by such action must be taken into account. If the Earth is held sacred and all Life is held sacred, then one must proceed with utmost caution and in the proper manner when making determinations involving the alteration of a natural habitat. This would seem a monumental task for even a highly telepathic peo-*

*ple. It was the function of the holy men known as the Earth Keepers.*

*There did come to be those who would act in the capacity of the medium, those who could separate from the physical self and bond with the physical elements of a particular landscape. These holy men, upon return to the reality of their physical bodies, would then render their determinations. Under the One Law there must be adequate habitat for all our relations to flourish as do we. The Earth Keepers, holy men and women of the One Law, were charged with the responsibility of safeguarding the sanctity of the Earth Mother. These held ultimate authority over human activity upon the land. These early Keepers were more powerful than the elders who sat upon the Great Council, for even the Great Council did defer to them.*

*Under the One Law, that which belongs to Creator is not for man to own unto himself. Such things may be utilized by man, but only when done in a manner consistent with One Law principles. It was the Earth Keepers who did determine where the people could gather, camp, hunt, grow or build. They knew good places where people could dwell in harmony with all around them. They knew the sacred places for prayer and healing. They were the keepers of the great Earth energy place, the sacred land of the one circle, that which was Atlantia.*

*If the people wished to build a community, construct dwelling places or plant crops in a particular area, an Earth Keeper had to be brought in and consulted. The Keeper did study the proposal and inspect the area in question. He did then choose a place to seat himself and meditate in order to commune with the natural Life forces and elements thereof. The physical vehicle might remain so seated for many days as the Keeper, gone out from same, integrated with the Life forms around him. Thus he became one with same in order to determine whether the area was receptive to the proposal. All aspects of Life and the sustainment thereof were taken into consideration.*

*Upon his return he was bathed and massaged with fragrant oils. He was given food and drink, and then he rested. The next day he did call together all concerned parties to announce his determination. Either the land was receptive to the needs of the people, or the land had to be honored and left unaltered.*

*At times, when a proposal was accepted, the Earth Keepers did provide specifications as to procedure and degree of alteration and did perform rituals, purification and prayer ceremonials. So it was in the early times of Atlantean history. As all things, this would come to change as Atlantean civilization and population did grow.*

*Those who would be Earth Keepers did display their special talents and abilities even before their initial nature-walk experience. Educators did take note of those individuals predisposed toward communication of such magnitude along the full spectrum of physical experience. A youth who demonstrated mastery of the nature-walk experience did attract the attention of high priests and the Great Council. Such youth would be offered the opportunity to train their abilities and prepare to enter service in the priesthood as Earth Keepers.*

*In the land of Atlantia there came to be constructed the Temple of the One. This complex did house the functions of the high priests and the Great Council or High Council. Herein, and going out from here, were the Keepers of the Land.*

*So it was in the early times of Atlantean history until the arrival of our relatives from the stars. These did bring a time of great change for Atlantis and her people. New ideas introduced at this time did begin to erode the old traditions. With the advent of the new age many old One Law taboos concerning the alteration of natural Earth habitats became relaxed or modified. The Order of the Word expanded its program at this time.*

*Poseidon and those descended from him proceeded to alter the face of the Atlantia land. There was the encirclement, and there did arise temples, resi-*

*dences and places of government. The city did grow and Atlantia became the heart of the great city of Poseidon.*

*There did come to be a new religious temple constructed, the Temple of the Sun. The rising sun was the symbol of a new age for mankind. It did represent a new dawn of unlimited possibility, born out of contact with our star relations. The Temple of the Sun distorted the truths of the One Law. That the Creator intends abundance for all was translated to mean growth, expansion and unlimited prosperity for Atlantis and her people. The new religion did take hold and did grow, for many put their faith in technology and progress and turned away from the spiritual truths of the One Law.*

*Under the old-order royal lineage, the Earth Keepers of the Temple of One were no longer the only determiners of land proposals. Documented approval had to be obtained from religious and government authorities after consultations with same. At this time Atlantean law did require not only religious authorization but consent from the king as well before proceeding with land development. Factors were taken into consideration which were other than those spiritual, such as the accommodation of population growth, the development of mobile transportation and the growth of other city centers upon the isle. Religious authorization could be obtained through the Temple of One or the Temple of the Sun.*

*There were those who did continue to follow the One Law, and these did still abide by the determinations of the Earth Keepers. But there were many others who sought approval from the Temple of the Sun first or after their proposal had been turned down by the Temple of One. The Temple of the Sun did not consider the Life force and the natural elements of areas proposed for development. Its main agenda was growth and economic expansion. Therefore, proposals were more readily accepted at the Temple of the Sun.*

*So it was in the days before the Great Cataclysm brought to a close the Lemurian age and the early Atlantic age. There would be a return to the Law of One as Atlantis (now Poseidia, Arlyan and Og) and her people did recover from the destruction. I have no more to relate on this subject at this time.*

# The Field of Aeronautics

*Greetings. I would speak at this time concerning the aeronautical development which took place during the three ages of Atlantic history. I would relate that which did concern the technology and utility of same, and would begin so by providing a descriptive account of those airborne vehicles.*

*Aircraft then were as varied in size, shape and function as are those of present experience and understanding. There were small machines for personal transportation and large craft designed for the transport of passengers and materials over vast distances. Examine current aeronautical history and there see a reflection of the evolution and development of that science in Atlantic antiquity. The fundamentals of lift, direction and stability in the air have always been and will never alter. Therefore, evolving in much the same manner, the aircraft of ages past would appear similar in many ways to those of present experience. The greatest differences between the Atlantic and present aeronautic technologies would be found within the power and propulsion systems. In this respect, the two would be worlds apart, so to speak.*

*Earliest Atlantean aircraft were of a configuration similar to the balloon types of the nineteenth century. Those of this type did measure from 14 to 38 feet in diameter. These measurements would relate to the enclosure, or envelope, for the containment of heated air. Early aircraft such as these were dependent on the generation of heat to produce lift. There were two ways to generate such heat. One way was through controlled ignition of flammable gases; the other was through the use of electrical elements. The resultant heat was directed through ducts to the containment envelope. That which did make for control as well as all mechanical components were suspended below the envelope.*

*From the balloon types did evolve the airship, the design and construction of which was similar to the dirigibles of present understanding. Such craft were dependent upon gases within a compartmentalized containment structure for lift. Located below the containment structure, either as part of or connected underneath same, were the electrical, mechanical and propulsion systems and the control compartment. There were compartments for either passenger or material transport. Early airships were propelled through the use of the internal combustion engine.*

*The airships were capable of traveling long distances between the mother island and the far lands. They did offer comfort and service to travelers, and they did transport huge loads of trade goods. They were the great wonders of the air during the early Atlantic age, yet they were susceptible to certain atmospheric conditions under which they could be very difficult to control. These great ships were also very slow in speed.*

*These early types did evolve yet further. Addressing the airship's stability and control problems, engineers did incorporate a more aerodynamic approach to airship design. They did utilize a more winglike construction over that of the obese, cylindrical design. This was found to reduce stability problems and improve directional control. These early "wings" were propelled through the use of internal combustion engines, but only until development of an early system of solar power came about. Through the use of quartz crystals, light was transformed into electricity. It was this which did power the engines that drove the propellers. Thus the wings came to rely on an early version of crystal power.*

*I would point out that other than the airship types, there did evolve those vehicles which did achieve lift by the action of airflow over the "aeroplanes." Early examples of this type incorporated several airfoil surfaces to produce lift. These would be very similar to the biplanes of present understanding. Later examples had but a single airfoil surface. Compartments for occupants, as well as all things electrical and mechanical, were contained within the body, or fuselage, of the craft. These aircraft types would appear similar in many ways to those of the first half of this present century.*

*Before the event of the first cataclysm, Atlantean aeronautic technology allowed for the transportation of passengers and materials to the far lands with ease. The occurrence of the Earth axial tilt did wipe away this science, along with the civilization and a majority of the people. This great cataclysm did cause the destruction of Lemuria, and the continent of Atlantis did break into smaller isles. For a great many years the sky would be void of Atlanteans and their machines.*

*Through centuries did the survivors heal and repopulate. With assistance from our interplanetary relations they did rebuild and progress, and Atlantis did once again take to the air in machines.*

*The redevelopment of aeronautical science was rapid. They did catch up with themselves as they had been before, and they did progress far beyond that. The birth of the empire did bring rapid advancement of aeronautic science. Atlantean engineers knew that efficient flight required solar power and crystal technology. Atlantis excelled.*

*I would speak of the use of solar energies in the propulsion of aircraft, the focus of solar energy to produce power. Light energy, focused and reflected through perfectly grown and faceted quartz crystals, can produce and amplify electrical power. In those ages past, such crystals were located within light amplification and projection devices inside the pyramid capstones. The solar light ray was reflected, amplified and projected through these devices. Intense, amplified rays of force were directed outward from these, to be received by focusing and amplification devices aboard the aircraft. Thus we did construct capstone devices in the various cities throughout Atlantis and in places in the far lands.*

*Onboard focusing receptors resembled a dish of reflective properties and did act as antennae. Controlled and directed by crystal chips in the control mechanism, the receptor device was able to hold itself in perfect alignment with the power source, be it the pyramid capstone or solar direct.*

*The focusing device was powered by electrical storage units onboard the aircraft.*

*Light energies received from the capstone source did generate power-up of aircraft mechanical systems and engines. Once airborne, the focusing receptor could remain directed upon the capstone source when in range of same, or receive energy from the sun. Thus the aircraft could "ride the beam" or "go solar direct."*

*The system was yet further advanced by the development of propulsion by means of air thrust. Improvements in crystal technology enabled us to increase the power output which emanated forth from the capstones. It did also become possible to separate and isolate the various light rays of the spectrum. We could also intensify same. Propulsion by means of air thrust did come about, resultant of these improvements.*

*This form of propulsion was dependent on light-spectrum separation and amplification to provide power-up and ignition of engines. A perfectly faceted diamond refraction device aboard the aircraft did separate the various spectral rays of light. These rays were directed into the various systems of the aircraft. A laser ray did superheat gases, which produced great force through the turbines. Thus was produced the jet stream of propulsion. When in cruise configuration the energy source was solar direct.*

*Thus Atlantis achieved the attainment of greater speeds and altitudes of flight. The speed of sound was achieved and exceeded. Aircraft of this type were capable of swift flights of short duration to the farthest reaches of the empire. The design and appearance of these craft was very aerodynamic, very sleek and modern, in your terms. These did vary in size, shape and function, as do those of present experience.*

*There are many similarities between the aeronautical development of Atlantis and the development of same in the present century. This is due to the fact that Atlantean technology has become incarnate in material form. There are many souls existent at this time, having been of Atlantean sojourn in those ages past. There is much of Atlantean influence in material form at present which accelerates technological development.*

*I would speak as concerns this entity's involvement in the field of aeronautics during those times long past. Involvement in the design of such aircraft had its beginnings within the Temple of Flight in the city of Poseidon during the age of the empire. There I did study and did eventually progress into advanced aeronautic science, primarily focused on airframe design. Working for a period upon aircraft of the propeller-driven types, I had great interest in research and development of the larger, farther ranging examples.*

*In a later period my own interest and attention turned to research being conducted into the greater speeds and higher altitudes of the jet-thrust aircraft. Before departure from the aeronautic field of experience, I had become involved in research concerning outer atmospheric control and stability in the development of craft for travel in space.*

*I would relate an explanation of the reasons for my discontinuance of activities in the aeronautic field. Government-sponsored programs increased their funding at the temple. Programs at the Temple of Flight and at the Temple of Defense did become more closely associated. Government realized the usage of aircraft as a diplomatic tool. The military realized the usage of aircraft as a weapons platform. To these, aviation was for use in the event of conflict somewhere within the vast empire, as a means of imposing Atlantean will. Aircraft were deployed against those perceived as enemies of Atlantean influence and expansionism. This science, as utilized by government and the military for the enforcement of Atlantic will, became that to which this entity could no longer continue to contribute, as that energy is contrary to the Law of One.*

*The advances in speed and altitude, the science of aerodynamic design, the involvement in space research — these things held wonder and fascination for this being. The joy of continued efforts in this field dissipated as I came to question the usage of that technology for the purposes of greed and destruction. I did then find refuge and contemplation at the great Temple of the One Law and remained there for some years in study and meditation. I did then resume the priesthood and did eventually teach in the old way.*

*Atlantean aeronautical research and development programs continued on, with resultant advancements and achievements. For example, your American astronauts were not the first to travel to the lunar surface. Utilizing solar energy, Atlantis sent her lunar exploration vehicles there many ages in the past. Physical evidence of same there remains. American lunar exploration would have come close to an Atlantean geological research site near the area known as Fra Mauru. The American lunar program was brought to a close due to the inability to guarantee that communications could be effectively censored. Know that ancient Atlantean aeronautic science and technology are being utilized this day by the Sons of Belial to produce new "defensive" aircraft, the existence of which are unknown but to a very few.*

*Crystal and light technology is presently missing from the equation, be it for aeronautic, automotive, electrical or any number of various power applications. Though the technology is there, it is suppressed by the powers that be in favor of continued dependency on obsolete systems — this due to the great amount of wealth generated by same. I have no more to relate at this time.*

# Sound, Image and the Misuse of Technology

*I would speak at this time concerning the subjects of Atlantean music and sound technology. Atlantis did excel in the art of music. There were the creation and performance of magnificent musical works, and these did encompass a wide spectrum of stylistic variation. Many were the great performance halls and amphitheaters, all of which were acoustically perfect, wherein great artists did perform their works for the public. There were also highly evolved recording facilities for the reproduction of musical works. There was the great Temple of Sound in the city of Poseidon, wherein did take place the study of all aspects of the science of sound.*

*There was a great multiplicity of composers, musicians and musical forms. Atlantean musicians utilized wind, string and percussion instruments as well as those electronically produced and such as were computer-generated. We Atlanteans did define music in a broader sense than as finds acceptance this day. The sonic tonalities of the great Ascidgean-Ra would sound strange to your ears, while various popular recordings of that period would sound comparable to some contemporary forms. The raga music of India is comparable to a form of early Atlantean spiritual music often heard within the Temple of the One Law. This musical form was reintroduced into the modern age during the third century* B.C. *Many of the principles and sounds of the raga reflect the One Law, in that this music incorporates the natural laws in its structure.*

*Through experience one finds that music has the power to alter the consciousness and the emotions. It can trigger thoughts, memories and scenes within the mind's eye. It can induce what would be described as a dreamlike state of consciousness in which the mind's eye is focused on a far and distant point other than that of the here and now.*

*When you listen to music, it soothes or stirs the mind and body deep within the self. It is felt and it affects you. The mind's eye envisions the music. One becomes a part of the music, the part that is in the here and now, in the moment, the instant . . . because that is the realm of music. One is carried along the space-time continuum, borne aloft by the intricate vibrational patterns of melody, rhythm and harmonics, thus attuning to the natural flow of all physical matter, to the All That Is! Such is the power of sound.*

*The Law of One teaches that principles of sound vibration are related to the natural laws of the universe. On the spiritual level, music or sound, aligned with the space-time continuum or the working universe, can promote vibrational harmony between the physical and nonphysical realms, thereby opening doorways of communication and interaction.*

*All that exists in the physical realm consists of a vibrating molecular structure. Therefore the mind and body are merely vibrating atoms, all parts vibrating at different frequencies and performing various functions. All must be in harmony for the one to function at full capacity. When one physical aspect goes dissonant, it can throw the entire system out of balance. The result is manifest as physical, emotional or psychological dysfunction.*

*In Atlantis, science and the art of music came together in the study of sound. Ascidgean-Ra was a great musician and composer who was known throughout Atlantis during the early Atlantic age.*

*He was the first to note the correlation between various sound frequencies and the vibrational frequencies of the chakral points of the physical body. These are the centers of Life energies which balance the physical and spiritual self. Ascidgean-Ra did show that specific sounds and frequencies, directed and amplified through quartz crystals, can effect change in the electrophysiology of the body. In other words, people can be tuned like one would tune a musical instrument.*

(The word *chakra* is Sanskrit for "wheel of fire." The seven major chakras can be envisioned as seven spinning wheels, each of which is of a different color, pattern and vibration. They are situated along the primary nerve groupings of the seven major endocrine glands.)

*Through the manipulation of various tonal frequencies, it is possible to alter the consciousness. Various combinations of sound also affect the auric field. Finely attuned administration of sound-wave frequencies can influence and alter thought, induce out-of-body experience and stimulate physical healing.*

*And so there came to be those who created music as art and those who studied sound as a science. This did advance, and found numerous applications. Know that just as there are the positive applications, there are those which are negative as well.*

*If sound can expand the consciousness, advance the spiritual and even heal the physical, then so too can it be utilized to inflict pain, numb the emotions or program thought and affect behavior.*

*I would speak as concerns the transmission of information through the atmosphere, or through a conductor, to a reception monitor, that which is presently understood as television. This was brought about in Atlantis before the first great cataclysm, and did emerge again in the period before the birth of the empire. Atlanteans did listen to broadcast transmission of sound and view images on receivers very similar to those of present experience. The technology was very much the same then as is at present. This medium was utilized as a source of information and a means of communication. It was utilized for education, as a link to the temples and government, and also for the purpose of entertainment.*

*Before he did assume the title of emperor, Amillius conspired through the Council of Three to bring about state control of the broadcast industry — this to control commercial interests and open the way for "advancements." Know that as the Sons of Belial took control of the medium then, so have their modern counterparts taken control of same at present. These realize the power of this technology as relates to mass thought and behavioral control.*

*During the second Atlantean age sound-wave technology was employed to anesthetize entire populations into submission. The empire's population-control program involved sound-frequency generation to effect thought control in the far lands. This was an important factor, critical to the progression of the empire's expansionist agenda.*

*During the height of the empire's reign, there was three-dimensional, interactive broadcast and projection. There was the transmission of sound which would seem to emanate from nowhere, yet from everywhere at once. There were recordings and equipment which could reproduce events as if those events were taking place in reality.*

*Before the event of the second great cataclysm, Atlantis could project great armies and weapons at an enemy, who would not be able to discern reality from illusion. This enabled Atlantean occupation forces to move in and eliminate all opposition with ease. This was a very powerful weapon system, a good example of the misuse of power and technology by the Sons of Belial during the height of the empire's reign. This weapon was to be utilized in full-scale deployment in a great attack upon what this day is known as China. This was to be phase two of a planned invasion of that land.*

*Countless were the applications to which the*

*Atlantean people did employ sound and image technology in those ages past. As it was in Atlantis long ago, many elements of human-control technique and technology are blatantly evident in American society at present. Living in urban and suburban areas, most are unconscious of the effects of same upon themselves.*

*Many suffer from highly elevated stress levels, physical ailments and dysfunction in family and other relationships. They find Love, happiness and contentment elusive; many feel lost and hopeless. These suffer constant psychological and emotional conditioning as well, the result of population-control techniques developed by ancient Atlanteans ages ago. This is not new technology, but is in fact ancient knowledge. Know that this is a real and present danger confronting spiritual progression, free thought and positive human growth and potential this day! I would end the transmission at this point.*

# THE FIRST CATACLYSM

*I would address the subject of the first great cataclysm, that which destroyed Lemuria and was the first such global destruction experienced by modern man. I refer to that which was brought about by the forces generated as the result of a planetary movement, a shifting upon Earth's axis.*

*Near the end of the Lemurian/early Atlantic age, there were wise old Lemurian priests who foretold of the coming global cataclysm. Before the event, there were those Lemurians who sailed to Atlantis and other parts of the world, bearing this message. However, these warnings went largely unheeded by Atlanteans, for their technology and science gave no warnings of such a coming event.*

*The appearance in Atlantis of our relatives from the stars had been heralded as the beginning of a new age for mankind. At the time of the event, Atlantis was at the height of its old order, its golden age, under the reign of the descendants of great Poseidon. The promises of the Temple of the Sun, those of prosperity and abundance, had blossomed to fruition. From the rule of Poseidon forward, the One Law declined as Atlantis embraced material abundance, technology and science.*

*The technology available to Atlantis at that time, although capable of monitoring atmospheric and geologic conditions and events, was incapable of providing advance warning of the axial tilt. The same held true for our space relations. How does one predict such an event? As did the ancient priests of the One Law, by acknowledgment of the messages spoken through the Earth's many voices! She speaks to us; we have but to listen. The situation at that long-ago time does mirror that of present experience. It is time to heed the warnings of the Earth and the prophets!*

*I would describe the event of the first cataclysm. This came upon us suddenly and without warning. First, great storms took shape and raged over the lands, followed by great volcanic activity and earthquake, and the land of Mu did fold in upon itself. Then the great waters of the ocean did sweep over this land. All of the people thereupon did cease physical being, and the land of Mu existed no more. The Atlantean land suffered great upheaval and flooding, though not to the degree as did the land of Mu. Many a soul did cross over into Spirit form during the event, and all of the many beautiful homes and buildings of the city of Poseidon did crumble and fall down. The great pyramid temples did crack and break, for the mountains moved and the Earth opened up. Then great waters of the ocean did sweep over the canals and through the city. So did everything become broken and all was strewn about, for everywhere there was great violence. The Atlantean continent did break up and become several islands, which would come to be known as Poseidia, Arlyan and Og.*

*All over the Earth there was upheaval and reaction until she did begin to settle after the event. A great number of beings did depart the Earth experience. Star relations, caught unaware upon the planet's surface, did cease physical existence. Those above the Earth did suffer as well, as their programs did suddenly go off-line, so to speak.*

*After the event, those few Atlantean survivors in the far places found themselves cut off from their homeland and knew not the fate of their people. Those few who did survive upon the home islands found themselves without civilization, technology or medicine. These did find great difficulty in meeting basic needs. The Earth and mankind began the process of healing, which would go on for many centuries. The people did return to old tribal ways, and there was reawakening to that of the Law of One. They came together in the sacred circle and offered prayers into their ceremonial fires. They came to live in harmony with the Earth once more.*

*Many hundreds of years did pass as the Earth and Atlantis healed, becoming vibrant and healthy again. The people did gather at the ruins of the site where had stood the great circles and the city of Poseidon. There they did begin to clear, repair and rebuild. This period of time came to be known as the great reconstruction, when the Atlantean people came together in rebuilding their civilization.*

*There came the first of those who did return to Atlantis from the far-off places where they had dwelled since before the event. More did follow, of those who returned home, to the mother isles. So too did those of our relations from the stars reappear in the sky. These did aid and assist in the rebuilding and reorganization. The people did clear and tend the center of the city and the Temple of the One Law was repaired. They did rebuild the heart of Atlantis and the seat of government, the city of Poseidon.*

According to Tiagorrah, the first global cataclysm

took place around 48,000 B.C. The cause of this great destruction upon the Earth was a shift of the planet upon its axis. Atmospheric, geologic and oceanic reactions were severe and widespread. Many died, and technology was lost to the world.

Major Earth changes have been predicted to take place in our own near future. We are already experiencing reactions by the Earth to the burdens imposed on her by mankind. Is what happened to Atlantis 50,000 years ago a preview of what is to come?

*Strange weather conditions and events shall intensify globally. Know that from this point, there is no turning back of that which has been set into motion . . . unless immediate and decisive actions are taken on a global scale!*

The Earth will not sustain a truly global consumer society. We continue to consume ever more of the Earth's resources to feed the throw-away lifestyle which we have been programmed to accept from childhood by government, corporations, the media and the public education system. Our lives revolve around the production and consumption of "convenient" disposable goods. We give of our labor, health and freedom toward these goals, and the result is waste, pollution and enslavement for millions.

Although we know that the Earth's natural resources are finite, global consumption and pollution rates continually increase. Meanwhile, government and corporate leaders continue to conduct business as usual, seeking to go global in promoting the consumer mentality and lifestyle. We cannot export all over the world the standard of living we have grown accustomed to here in America and other developed nations. Simple logic dictates that not everybody everywhere needs to own automobiles, personal computers, VCRs and cellular telephones. The whole world does not need fast food, shopping malls and minivans! Besides the problem of finite resources, a global consumer society would literally suffocate in its own waste, as pollution levels would be intolerable.

Our present system measures economic well-being according to how much is produced and consumed. Contemporary Sons of Belial have the majority of people believing that material possessions and conveniences are necessities which bring peace, happiness and contentment. The more you spend and consume, the better for the economy of all. The truth is, the more you play the game, the more you contribute to the problem.

Those who talk global economics, the multinational corporations, continue to conduct themselves quite like pigs at the Earth trough, gorging themselves through the pillaging of the natural environment and the economic enslavement of their fellow human beings. I myself do not consider this to be progress. It is this writer's opinion that such behavior on the part of these corporate giants contributes to the decay of the human race and the planet Earth. It does not improve people's lives or help to heal the planet in any way. Actually, I see it more as mindless insanity.

What is happening to the Earth is a crime, a crime perpetrated by the contemporary Sons of Belial, and most people follow along like sheep, living in ignorance and oblivious to the urgency of the situation. Man is the caretaker of the Earth. We have failed in this.

What is to be done about the problem? What are "they" going to do about it? If we leave it up to elected officials and world leaders — little to absolutely nothing. Their purpose is to sustain the beast. The more they contribute to the growth of the beast, the better job they've accomplished in office. If the general population does not acknowledge the problems at hand and make fundamental changes in themselves and their society, then the Earth will make the changes for us.

Immediate measures need to be taken to reverse the present drain on the Earth and her resources. The token measures taken by our leaders in these areas are too little. As yet, I don't believe that our leaders or our society itself are willing to make the necessary changes. However, the pollution and destruction must end now, for the Earth changes have already begun.

*The Earth Mother does indeed react to stress in much the same way as the human body. She develops symptoms, and these would occur as strange weather patterns, rumblings and movement of the land. When she does indeed respond, it will be as a sleeper in the night. She will stir and stretch and adjust her position.*

Tiagorrah uses the phrase, "mirror that of present experience," when he speaks of unheeded warnings. When the Lemurian priests warned Atlanteans of impending Earth changes 50,000 years ago, the Atlantean attitude was similar to that of many today. If scientists, geologists and meteorologists have no indications to support any fears of a global catastrophe in the near future, then there is nothing to worry about. Though many modern-day prophets are listening to the Earth and telling us that she is getting ready to react, they are not being acknowledged.

The time is now! We *must* listen to the prophets! If we are committed toward unrestrained global economic and industrial expansion — the proliferation of what Ralph Nader calls the consumer mentality — and the continued disregard for the natural environment, then we are committed to a replay of the first great cataclysm which befell the Earth 50,000 years ago.

*The impending Earth changes are the result of mankind's overburdening of the Earth. She will be taxed into activity. The result will be a release of energy; there will be cleansing and renewal of the Earth. Look around you and hear the messages. Heed the warnings of the ancient Grandmother!*

According to Tiagorrah, "the Earth will be taxed into activity." The difference between the first cataclysm and the Earth changes predicted for our future is that humanity today precipitates the event through its disregard of One Law principles — that all Life is sacred, that the Earth is our mother, that Love is the most powerful force in the universe, and that Spirit is within all things. All is interconnected under the Law of One!

# The Birth of an Empire

*Know that the history of Atlantis is long and complex. Information and details covering all of the many aspects of same would require an immense undertaking and a great number of years in its completion. I will focus upon that which is relevant to the experience of those incarnate in the present, that which is relevant to a realization and understanding of the present state of world affairs. I would speak as concerns the formation, or the coming into being, of the Atlantean empire, or that known then as the great world power. I would relate the events which did lead to the development of same.*

*Through time did the people of Atlantis progress in the reconstruction of their civilization. Three thousand years after the event of the first cataclysm, the first oceangoing craft were primitive wind-driven vessels. These carried the first who ventured to return to the oceans to reconnect with the far lands. From these beginnings did the art of shipbuilding reemerge. In similar fashion did other technologies find reemergence. Our relations from the stars returned to our skies. They sent down their people, who did aid Atlantis in recovery.*

*Know that 5000 years after the event, the city of Poseidon had been returned to its former condition in many aspects. Within those long years had Atlantis healed and grown. She was once again at a point of progress and technology. Her people had reinvented their technologies of transportation and communication. The lanes of travel and trade were once again opened to the far places of the Earth. Once again did Atlanteans venture to the places you now know as Africa, India, Egypt, Europe and the Americas.*

*There did come to be a new religious and spiritual order known as the Temple of the Sun. In cities across the isles of Atlantis, new temples came to be constructed which did belong to this new order. As the sun represented new beginnings, growth and abundance, so did the new Temples of the Sun encourage material abundance and consumerism, progress and expansion. These did promote ambi-*

*tion and lust for power and influence, that which did root the consciousness in the present moment of the physical experience. Thus, many gathered in those temples in expectation of abundance and prosperity. These forces were contrary to One Law consciousness, and there did evolve separations and deep divisions between the people. So did the negative elements begin to exert themselves and the One Law begin to fade.*

*By the time period of approximately 40,000 B.C., the people of the Atlantic isles had grown in their number. Their society had likewise grown and become more complex. They did bring changes to their environment as their society and their cities did expand. As their industry and technology did grow, so too did that which would eventually erupt in confrontation. Atlantis was then going through political change, and there was much confusion concerning government. They came to question the old system of council government. Many claimed that it was no longer effective to serve the modern needs of the people. This was a time of great transition for Atlantis.*

*Those of the One Law, the Sons of Belial and our relations from space did maneuver and manipulate Atlantean public opinion in order to gain the support necessary to carry out their agendas. The Pleiadians did support the installment of an old-*

*order form of government, having been comfortable with that arrangement in the past. The followers of the One Law did support the way of the One road and continued council government. The Sons of Belial did support a strong central government, economic growth and expansion, and a "defensive" military establishment.*

*The failing and endangered High Council did then agree to conduct a series of hearings, which I shall refer to as the core negotiations, or that which did concern a cooperative reorganization. From out of these proceedings there came the establishment of the Council of Three, also known as the Triad government, that which did represent compromise in the system. The Council of Three acted as the ultimate authority over all matters of government policy. Council members did consist of a people's advocate who was elected by the people and acted "according to their will"; the Advocate of the One Law; and the advocate in representation of the Sons of Belial and the Temple of the Sun.*

*Whether or not this system was an improvement over that of the old was the question which did bring about yet further argument and division. The numbers did grow of those who believed that this government, though an improvement, was still inadequate to serve the needs of Atlantis in an effective manner. Opposition to the system did grow as debate between the elements escalated. Thus, due to argument and confrontation, the system did come to be even more ineffectual.*

*Resistance to Atlantean influence had begun to build in the far lands due to continual policy and treaty changes concerning trust and fairness in trade relations. Trade with Atlantis had become increasingly one-sided, to the point where Atlantis only did benefit from the relationship. In the lands known this day as India and Tibet, which had once been greatly influenced by Lemuria, did the people come to resist Atlantis. These lands and former outposts had maintained their independence and had managed their own affairs during the earlier times of the old order. Atlantis in those times had sent out her representatives and ambassadors to those lands. She did have her embassies there in the times before the event of the first cataclysm. I would that you understand this: that when Atlantis did act under the observance of the One Law as a foundation for international relations, then did she experience peaceful, cooperative and beneficial involvement. Only when the elements of greed, ego and corruption did enter in was there a development of resistance among the people of those lands.*

*The Sons of Belial gathered public support for the design and production of a defensive naval force. Their representatives and operatives managed to initiate design and construction of armed ships of the sea. At the time, ships of the air were mainly giant dirigible types, which could carry aloft many people. They were slow, lumbering beasts. However, these did serve well as observation platforms. When armed and tested, they also proved to be adequate weapons platforms. Atlantis did bring together an air force which consisted of a number of these giant ships. They also deployed many small, winged aircraft, which had proven to be faster and more maneuverable. When armed with weapons, these were found to be much more accurate and deadly than the larger and slower airships. Production of an oceangoing vessel which could accommodate, transport and deploy these aircraft was commissioned by factions in the government.*

*The Sons of Belial did come to influence a majority of those in high places to support a new government. This new government would be strong and determined, concerning itself firstly with the growth and development of Atlantis and her people. These did envision Atlantis going forth in the world to develop a new world order of peace and prosperity.*

*I would speak at this time concerning a great figure in Atlantean history. I would speak at this time of Amillius. This was a highly evolved incarnate being who was a high priest at the Temple of the One Law in the city of Poseidon. For a great many years did Amillius conduct himself as such, but then it did come to pass that he did find a grand new avenue of experience in politics. During the course of that experience, Amillius did come to be seduced by materialism and power, and by the political, religious and — more importantly — the material and monetary influences of the Sons of Belial. Amillius was appointed by the Sons of Belial to sit upon the Triad government as advocate in representation of the Temple of the Sun.*

*The elements involved did conspire, and it did come to pass, that there was further conflict. Through the maneuverings of Amillius, the Triad government did collapse. Amillius did then go forth and force public issue on the establishment of a new order of government. Thirty-eight thousand years before Christ there occurred the overthrow of the Council of Three and the beginnings of that which would become the great Atlantic empire. Amillius did declare himself to be the head of the new government, proclaiming that "one head upon the shoulders of Atlantis will better serve the people than three!" He did so with the full support of the Sons of Belial, the military and the industrial elements, but he was challenged by the One Law temple leaders.*

*Having already affected public opinion and being confident of the people's support, he did call for elections to take place. The elections did result as expected, and so Amillius did officially become ruler of the new Atlantean government. The way was then clear for the establishment of the new world order.*

*The first act of the new government was to send out its naval fleet to the far lands of the Earth. Thus the Atlantean navy presented itself and ceremoniously demonstrated its abilities to the people in those places — this much the same way as did the great white fleet of Theodore Roosevelt with which you are familiar. This early naval force would be considered primitive by later standards, yet no other people could effectively repel or resist Atlantean weaponry at that time. So it was that Atlantis came to declare dominion over the lands and peoples where early Atlantis had once had her outposts. These did now come under the "protection" of the empire.*

*It was declared that Atlantean rule would most certainly be beneficial for the peoples of these lands. Great Atlantis offered them advances in medicine, education, industry and trade, and benefits from Atlantean culture and art. They were assured that there was no end to the wonderful things that Atlantis could bestow upon them — should they peacefully accept Atlantean generosity and cooperate fully with their benefactors! There was little resistance. The fact that Atlantean ships sat offshore and Atlantean aircraft flew overhead did convince most who would resist to cooperate instead.*

*With this action, Atlantis did bring about great change in the world. Those who had been ambassadors became acting governors over the far lands and peoples. Where there was resistance, Atlantis did concentrate her forces. Troops landed and occupied those areas. The new Atlantean government, with its ships and airplanes, with its soldiers and governors in place in the far lands, now had the empire secured. So was the Atlantean empire born.*

*Once Amillius was emperor, the stage was set for great Atlantean growth and power in the Earth. Immediately there were initiated new programs for research and development of new technologies. Our relations from the stars did cooperate with top Atlantean researchers, engineers and scientists in many areas. So began the expansion of the empire Atlantis, the great power.*

*Thus began a new era of progress and prosperity for the Atlantean people. Ships and aircraft were produced which could travel greater distances at faster speeds. There were systems in place which were very similar to your present public transportation systems. The people of that long past time did travel out from Poseidia, Arlyan and Og to far lands of the Earth with ease. The economy expanded, and*

*Atlanteans experienced unprecedented growth and development.*

*There on the isle of Poseidia, on the Bay of Parfax, the city of Poseidon grew to a level of magnificence and splendor which has yet to be equalled. Within its walled enclosure there were great temple pyramids, luxurious residences, beautiful gardens, parks and wilderness areas. A fitting capital for the new world order! The civilization of Atlantis did eventually reach a level of intellect, sophistication and technological expertise far beyond that of present development. The Atlantic empire did expand itself nearly worldwide. I have no more to impart at present.*

# The New Atlantis

*Greetings. At this time I would focus upon that which is brought into manifestation within the society of the present day. I would speak as concerns this new Atlantis, the dominant society in the world today, which is the United States of America — this for the purpose of illumination, to shed light upon, so to speak, the situation confronting humanity at this current point of transition. The intent is to stimulate free thought and promote analysis of the following subject matter. I would that the readers grow in awareness and understanding of same. I would that there be awakening. Know that the message pertains not only to the United States; it does relate as well to similar technological societies world-*

*wide.*

*So it was that in the earlier part of the seventeenth century, there began to increase the influx of ancient souls who in ages past had experienced incarnation on this Earth as Atlantean. These did bring in with them deep soul-level remembrances of those times. Thus, there took place a corresponding influx of ideas and technologies long absent from the face of the Earth. Much did find reintroduction into physical reality. This migration of souls into being did accelerate, and accordingly, so did what you presently refer to as progress.*

*This twentieth century has witnessed such tremendous technological development that the present society cannot adjust to the changes such rapid advancement necessitates. There are many resultant effects. One is an acceleration of the time-compression effect. Thus it appears that there is less time, shorter distances and a faster pace to Life. This unusual phenomenon truly exists and does intensify.*

*Impressive is modern industrial ingenuity and invention! One is presently confronted with an endless variety of goods and services, all designed to improve the lifestyle and to make Life more comfortable, effortless and pleasant for all — or so it may appear. Presently, people have become so dependent upon conveniences that total anarchy would ensue in the absence of same. Mankind has once again allowed itself to be dominated psychologically, socially and economically. Once again, people have grown apart from each other, all of nature and the Creator. Thus freedom and spirituality are diminished while the negative forces of the sons of greed grow ever more powerful.*

*Presently, as in the ages of Atlantis, the followers of the Law of One must stand against the forces of the sons of greed and corruption, power and manipulation — the Sons of Belial! Know that the polarization intensifies.*

*I would speak of this present day and the reemergence of elements of these factions within the collective experience. Know that the sons of greed and corruption diligently labor toward their own self-serving aspirations of power and dominance. These have power over industries and government, they control the economy and manipulate the people.*

*The American government, which from its inception has been proclaimed as one that is "of the people, by the people and for the people," does not function as such. The "great American experiment" of freedom, liberty and justice was in reality an ingenious propaganda campaign. At present, freedom, liberty and justice degenerates increasingly — this being accelerated under the time-compression effects.*

*I would speak of present-day corporate leaders who discard their obligations to community, to humanity, to Life and to Earth. Their profit and wealth increase greatly while living standards decrease for the many. Their representatives promote lesser government for efficiency's sake, but lesser government can be translated as meaning greater freedom to exploit the people and the natural environment. Thus what you would term capitalism, unregulated and unrestrained, produces simply another system under which very few reap what the many labor to sow.*

*The twentieth-century dictators acted on the premise that the key to power was military superiority. At the end of this twentieth century it is accepted that the key to power is economic in nature — this now that technology allows for global communication and transaction. The Sons of Belial envision themselves as the dictators of the twenty-first century. They are those who divide people against one another according to culture, race, country and religion as well as social and economic status. These have no ethics, and operate only on the base-chakra level of consciousness. These are the Sons of Belial, who are driven by greed, endeavor only to profit and power, and are insatiable in their hunger. These Sons of Belial grow stronger behind the veil of progress and the facade of nor-*

*mality here in the present situation. Until humanity learns that greed is a truly negative force, comparable to a disease or an addiction, then the attainment of peace and enlightenment will continue to be a struggle. The present society encourages and promotes personal greed, and in so doing it accelerates its own dissolution.*

*As for the government of new Atlantis, the sons of greed promise change as relates to their political conduct. They promise to make right a variety of political, economic and social wrongs. Know that their ultimate goal is the attainment of yet greater personal wealth and power. Beware of these false prophets who profess diligence in their efforts toward the betterment of the social-economic conditions of your people. They would withdraw support for all art forms and from the education of children and young adults. They would withdraw aid for the elders, the poor, the sick and the hungry. In the name of the reduction of government regulation, they would forsake environmental protection and conservation, thus allowing increases in pollution and destruction of the natural environment. In the name of economic responsibility, they would extract ever more wealth and labor from the expanding number of citizens experiencing economic decline. Thus is fed the hunger of government and their industrial overlords.*

*Beware of terms such as global economy, global marketplace and global industry. Beware of the users of same. In all actuality, these phrases can be interpreted as referring to policies of global influence by the ruling elite. At the height of Atlantean expansionism, similar phrases were as much in fashion as those this day. Current political and industrial leaders hail the expansion of so-called democracy in areas of the world where communism has declined. Know that underlying their rhetoric of freedom and liberty rest their true ambitions toward the expansion of their own political and economic gain. The peoples of these areas have simply traded one form of exploitation for another.*

*Those who perpetuate the ancient goals and aspirations of the Sons of Belial are alive and well this day. These do experience unprecedented growth and prosperity as well as sure and steady progression toward their ultimate goal—that of global domination. Know that these seek nothing less than to resurrect the empire, Atlantis! They would have the power of the Temple of the Sun shine upon a one-world government, a global community, a new world order for the next millennium! These souls do envision no less than the rebirth of the Atlantic empire, much like the legendary phoenix rising.*

*Know that this day the Sons of Belial do control and direct the affairs of governments, religions, industries, trade and economic systems. They do control science and technology as well as all forms of the mass media. The highest and most powerful of these controllers do go about unseen, while their agents operate in disguise. Look to the highest seats of power and influence, and there sitting, see their operatives! The high priests are few, their invisible manipulations progressing the ancient goals of Poseidon, Amillius and Belial. From the apex of the pyramid, the very capstone of the Temple of the Sun, leading down to the most oblivious of the masses, all is in place and proceeds according to plan.*

*I would speak of religious institutions, which have so misrepresented and distorted the teachings of the great messengers that religious totalitarianism is the norm for the so-called faithful. It is that which has been, and continues to be, the root cause of war, atrocity and infliction throughout this modern age — this perpetuated upon mankind by the religious hierarchies and their representatives and followers worldwide. It is the realization of such that compels the swelling number of truth seekers to turn away from these institutions and walk an independent pathway.*

*Through these truth seekers many aspects of the One Law find reemergence into being this day. These seekers of the truth do realize such One Law aspects as acknowledgment of the One Creator —*

*this no matter what name is bestowed upon same in various areas of the Earth, nor what manner of worship be practiced within differing cultures. They see such aspects as the acknowledgment of beauty in all peoples and all cultures, for all are one people, one human race upon the Earth. That which dwells within the physical form is truly sacred and so must be honored. They understand the sacredness of all Life forms with which they share existence in the world, that such is the gift of Creator, and that this must be honored no matter how great or small in the eyes of man. They know to acknowledge the sacredness of the living Earth, that it is the Earth Mother who sustains Life, and so she must be honored.*

*Many do not wish to acknowledge that which takes place in the reality of the present. These are content to continue Life concerned only with their own self-gratification and interests. Many at this time fail to consider the well-being of the whole. This goes against the great universal truth of the Law of One.*

*I would speak of the cycles of humanity and of that aspect of the One Law which pertains to the Oneness of all humanity. Know that everyone and everything are interconnected within the cosmic order of creation. Souls journey through the karmic cycles of existence with the ultimate objective of eventual reunion with Creator. On another level, the collective consciousness of all humanity similarly passes through karmic cycles, just as each does individually. Thus continues what can be termed as the cycles of humanity. Each individual contributes to the collective consciousness of the whole. One is both spiritual and material in the incarnate state. It is well to be on the spiritual pathway in this journey, but one must not forget one's responsibility as a part of the collective whole. It is this which did go wrong in Atlantis long ago and is that which now eats away at the integrity of the present society.*

*If we strive for spiritual progression without making a positive contribution to the collective whole, then we are contributing to the dissolution of the whole. One can contribute in a positive manner by consciously sending forth Love, compassion and healing in the form of thoughts and prayers directed toward fellow beings and the Earth. Thoughts are energy and words have power, but we must go beyond this.*

*Only through the realization of that which takes place in the world at present, only when there is acknowledgment of the manipulations and control of these forces, can those who seek find awareness and understanding. Then there will be a great awakening of consciousness and the lies will become transparent to all. Only then will these forces be nullified and brought into account. Christ consciousness, which is the Law of One, can raise the collective consciousness of mankind. Work now toward these goals, for the time grows near when this behemoth shall collapse. Spread the good news now about the Law of One. Touch others so that they might be awakened. Plant seeds now. The time for taking refuge in the countrysides draws near.*

If you look around you, Atlantis is reincarnated in our present society; it has returned through the reincarnation of its people. America today is the new Atlantis that the Founding Fathers of this country had envisioned. Taking another look at the history of America, from its discovery through the revolution, turned out to be rather interesting. It was as if Tiagorrah directed me to new information, and I learned many things I didn't know before.

> America was designed by Providence for the theater upon which mankind will make its true figure.
>
> — Samuel Adams

The United States of America grew from small agricultural beginnings to become the world's preeminent economic, technological and military force in less than two centuries! How did this come about?

*Progress has followed the course dictated by pre-*

*sent-day high priests of the Sons of Belial and the Temple of the Sun.*

First, I will address the subject of ancient Atlantean knowledge that has been handed down through the ages, since I believe it has a lot to do with the birth of the United States. Ancient knowledge of the One Law has been largely preserved within the traditions and spiritual wisdom of many tribal peoples all over the world. The ancient knowledge of the Temple of the Sun has been retained through the ages by what has become a vast network of secret societies. These organizations possess secret esoteric teachings known only to the highest initiates. These mystery schools can be traced all the way back to Atlantis. From there they spread to other parts of the Earth and formed ties with all the major religious institutions — Hebrew, Christian, Moslem etc. They existed in Egypt, Greece, Rome, Great Britain and, more recently, in the United States.

That Atlantis never existed because no traces of evidence survive to this day is exactly what the Sons of Belial support as the generally accepted public belief. The truth is that for those with the eyes and openness of mind to see, Atlantis most certainly did leave knowledge and evidence. This is in the influences left by Atlantis on the ancestors of modern-day tribal peoples worldwide and in the *records, texts and time capsules* which survive to this day and are kept from the public's knowledge.

*Such knowledge is in the keeping of, and kept secret by, the few high priests who know of its existence in the present human experience.*

Was prehistoric mystery wisdom, the Holy Grail, believed to have been kept by the Knights Templar? Could it have been the driving force behind human progression in this modern age? Was it the driving force behind the discovery of America and the foundation of the United States? Could it, at least in part, have played an important role in the sudden technological progression of the last two centuries?

Christopher Columbus had ties to a secret society known as the Temple of Christ, which had grown out of the Knights Templar. He had access to ancient knowledge in the form of maps. This, and sponsorship by the secret societies, made his discovery of America a success. As a result of this discovery, the old world began the massive colonization movement to the new world. Secret societies played a crucial role in the promotion and publicity which drove that movement and opened the floodgates. This is where the new Atlantis concept comes in.

Though not listed among them, one of the most influential of the Founding Fathers of the United States was Lord Chancellor of England, Sir Frances

Bacon. He was a high-level Rosicrucian who founded the Lodge of the Freemasons. He is credited as being the editor of the King James Version of the Bible. Strong evidence indicates that Bacon was the true author of the works of Shakespeare. He was a promoter of the scientific revolution of the seventeenth century, calling for "the total *reconstruction* of science" in order to *"restore* man to mastery over nature." Most people are unaware of the work he performed to further his great dream, the establishment of a new Atlantis. He wrote about it in a book entitled *The New Atlantis.* In this work Bacon describes his vision of a privileged elite, controlling secret knowledge, who nurture in a new land the rebuilding of the great Atlantean empire!

With the growth of Freemasonry in America, Bacon's dream of a new Atlantis progressed according to plan. By 1760 Freemasonry was agitating people against the British and implanting the idea that American liberty was God's cause and that God intended this land for the establishment of a new republic for His people. By 1773 American discontent was running high and the Masons were there to direct the resistance. They hosted the first act of revolution, the Boston Tea Party. The Masons were the moving force at all key points in the development and birth of the new Atlantis. All the leading generals of the Continental Army were Masons.

George Washington was a Master Mason. Franklin, Hamilton, Madison, Adams and many other Founding Fathers were Masons. In fact, 50 of the 55 members of the Constitutional Convention were Freemasons, as were 53 out of 56 signers of the Declaration of Independence!

Freemasons and their associates manipulated both sides in the American Revolution and then took control of the new government. With the signing of the Constitution, the dreams of Bacon, Washington and other Masons came true. While the ties with Britain had been cut, those between the secret society network and the new government grew ever stronger. Rule in America passed from control by the monarchy to control through democracy, which turned out to be control by the privileged elite. The next phase of the operation involved the promotion and proliferation of the concept of *manifest destiny.* This was the idea that nothing could stand in the way of the progression and expansion of this new nation — because it was the "will of God" that the new nation flourish.

This expansion required the extermination of the aboriginal inhabitants of the land. This was justified through the manifest destiny concept. Again, it was the will of God. This served two purposes: It freed up all the natural resources of the land, and it eliminated the One Law knowledge preserved by Native

American traditions and spiritual beliefs. For example, the following is excerpted from a letter written to President Franklin Pierce by Chief Seattle in 1855.

> The Great White Chief in Washington sends word that he wishes to buy our land. How can you buy or sell the land? The idea is strange to us. Every part of the Earth is sacred to my people. We know that the white man does not understand our ways. One portion of the land is the same to him as the next, for he is a stranger who comes in and takes whatever he wants. The Earth is not his mother but his enemy, and when he has conquered it, he moves on.
>
> The whites too shall pass. Perhaps sooner than other tribes. Continue to contaminate your bed and you will one night suffocate in your own waste. When the buffalo are all slaughtered, the wild horses all tamed, when the secret corners of the forest are heavy with the scent of many men, then what is left is the end of living and the beginning of survival.
>
> — Chief Seattle

There was no effort to learn anything from the Native American people or to truly make peace with them. They were simply seen as wild, heathen savages in the way of progress. Individuals, the likes of Andrew Jackson and George Custer, were made public heroes, whereas wise men such as Tecumseh, and later Red Cloud, were considered far less than human. The Law of One, preserved within the roots of Native American culture and spiritual belief, had to be eliminated. Nothing could be allowed to stand in the way of the objective, which was the western expansion of the Union, then the push forward to world influence and power.

Those who espoused liberty and freedom tried to wipe out an entire people, their traditions and spirituality. They looked upon other peoples as inferior. They enslaved the Africans. Those who professed independence and individuality brought about the Industrial Revolution and the enslavement of the masses. On the Great Seal of the United States you will find the words *Annuit Coeptis,* which translates as "He smiles upon our undertakings"; *E pluribus unum,* meaning "one out of many"; and *Novus Ordo Seclorum,* which translates as "announcing the birth of a new order of ages"—a new world order. You will also find a pyramid (representing the Temple of the Sun) and the "all-seeing eye." This blatant symbolism is an expression of those who hold power over this country and many others. It is the symbolism of the Sons of Belial.

They retain control of the masses by convincing them that they are powerless and have no control, that nothing can be done about it, and that's just the way it is. People believe that they have no power and so continue to plod along and remain with the program. They rely on some corporate entity to supply them with capital, in return for which they prostitute their bodies and minds. There are those who would like to effect change, but under the present system are too busy simply trying to earn a living and unable to do much else. Freedom and liberty in America today translates into what I call compensated slavery for millions of people. Sounds like this all came right out of George Orwell's *1984,* doesn't it? The point is, all is not what it would seem — or, as Henry Ford once said, "History is bunk!"

# The Law of One

*The Law of One was known among the people of Mu long before those of Atlantis. This was the original religion of a people who were, quite literally, connected to the Spirit world. The One Law was introduced to Atlantis through the visiting and transplanted Lemurians. Many of the priests of early Atlantis were Lemurian. Ultimately, the Lemurians had a pure form of the One Law, in that they experienced no development of the negative influence, as did Atlantis through the Sons of Belial. This explains why early relations from the stars viewed them as the more spiritually developed people.*

Where does one begin to explain something as

complicated, yet as simple, as the Law of One? Well, perhaps it is that something which many people spend their entire lifetimes trying to find. Maybe it is that something we are all looking for without knowing what it is or being able to define it. We remember it somehow, somewhere deep down inside. We have a longing for it and search for it out there in the physical world.

Tiagorrah says that we have soul memory of it. Soul memory is very different from our brain's facility for memory, for it is at the very core of our being. It is who we are, our talents and abilities, it is our nature and motivations. It is a part of our spiritual and physical makeup and can be accessed through the practice of meditation. We do not have to keep running around like chickens with their heads cut off, trying to find something that we cannot identify to fill the need in us that we cannot describe.

The One Law rings true for so many because they have been carrying it within themselves all along. What happens is that their soul memory is awakened, and enlightenment and understanding follow. If there is something missing in Life, if the world around us doesn't make sense, could it be because the Law of One has been repressed throughout our recorded history? Could it be that the Law of One is the missing something in our lives, in our communities, in our civilization?

> A human being is a part of the whole, called by us the universe, limited in time and space. He experiences himself, his thoughts and feelings as something separated from the rest — a kind of optical delusion of his consciousness. This delusion is a prison, restricting us to our personal desires and to affection for a few persons close to us. Our task must be to free ourselves from our prison by widening our circle of compassion to embrace all humanity and the whole of nature in its beauty.
>
> — Albert Einstein

These days there are many out there preaching their own interpretations of spirituality, from television evangelists to New Age gurus. There is the prevalent fear-based traditional Christianity, wherein God punishes, sinners go to hell, it's God's will, and we all need to be saved. Then there are the present New Age extremists who think only "good" thoughts, send out only "positive" vibrations and don't let anything "negative" intrude into their space. From the extreme left to the extreme right, the entire spiritual and religious spectrum can be daunting to the truth seekers. Trouble is, most religions demand total adherence to their own particular dogma, through which people wind up directing negative emotions at others, based on difference. It can be a vicious circle. With all these spiritual roads and no road map, how does one spiritually navigate?

I like to use this example. Tiagorrah brought it to my attention one day and I think it makes a very good illustration. For some reason you feel compelled to experience the spiritual channel and sense that it is on channel one. You presume that channel one is to be found right there on your television set. There's only one problem: there *is* no channel one on your television set! You've got 150 channels to choose from, but you can't find channel one! What's going on here?

*So does one presume to find God within the confines of organized religion, but most often one finds disillusionment with religious dogma instead.*

If you want to pick up channel one, know that you are perfectly able to do so, but not on your television set. You are the receiver, the amplifier, the reception point. *You* are channel one! Within you exists the order of the universe, the All That Is and your own direct line to creation and Creator. Jesus Christ is reported to have said, "The kingdom of heaven is within you." One Law consciousness can be accessed simply by directing your focus within.

Here is another example. Think of your conscious mind as a personal computer. The only information you can get out of it is the same information that has been programmed into it. Think of the subconscious mind as the Internet. When a computer makes contact with the Internet, it has access to a world of information. Any computer in the world can link to the Internet and access the same information. Similarly, the conscious mind, by way of the subconscious link, can access the superconscious, that part of us which is in tune with the All That Is.

*The thinking, rational mind can only utilize and act upon the information which it assimilates through sensory input. The deeper realms of the subconscious mind can access universal knowledge!*

When the conscious mind descends to the deeper levels of the subconscious, it can have access to this universal knowledge. This is an aspect of One Law truth; therefore, every two-legged personal computer in the world comes Internet-ready! You don't need an Internet provider! You don't have to pay for access to the spiritual Internet! Hallelujah!

We are all Spirits who possess a body and a mind. The physical body is merely a vehicle which the Spirit inhabits in order to experience Life on the Earth plane. When we believe that the body we inhabit is truly who we are as we are programmed to believe, then we are always searching outside ourselves for that elusive something we can't describe. We look to that promotion at the office or that new luxury car or a relationship with another person. We look for answers from other people whom we consider *authorities.*

The church preaches that it is the work of the devil when an individual goes outside of its established parameters to explore other spiritual avenues. Well, of course! If people discovered their own personal connection to God, to the All That Is, they wouldn't look to the Church as the intermediary between God and man, would they? Hence, the Church would be out of business; it would no longer be able to maintain its control over the masses!

We all inherit the ability to communicate directly with Creator and the Spirit world. We need to realize this. By meditating and going within, we are able to tap into soul memory. We can raise individual consciousness from its entrapment in the mundane trivia of the material world and reconnect with the Source. Therefore, each individual plays an important role in determining our future. The Spirit is the direct link to God because it is a part of God, just as each drop of water is a part of the ocean. Spirit is a part of all creation and the link to greater knowledge of the All That Is. We can have a better understanding of our lives, of why we are here and what we are here to do. Meditation is the key.

*As a radio tunes in to various frequencies of reception, so too does the conscious mind attune itself to various vibrational frequencies and other states of being. Once the inward journey has begun, what unfolds is awakening and understanding. What unfolds is the Law of One.*

Tiagorrah says that the Law of One is so complex that I could spend the rest of my Life writing about it, trying to explain it. He also says that it's so simple that any little child can understand it fully. The Law of One is the Law of Love. Jesus Christ is reported to have said, "A new commandment I give unto you, that you love one another. As I have loved you, that ye also love one another." The Love that Christ displayed was unconditional Love, One Law Love! Many aspects of the One Law can still be found in Christ's words; in fact, all of history's sacred messengers, from Christ to Krishna to White Buffalo Calf Woman, spoke about the various aspects of the Law of One. Unfortunately, as history attests, these messages have been altered by the Sons of Belial to meet their needs and purposes.

Life, Love, Earth and Spirit are the four major elements of the Law of One. Love is the single most powerful force in the universe, a positive force of unlimited potential! The effects of Love are cyclic in nature, in that the Love you send out comes back to you from others. The power of Love expands outward and is amplified in this way, so the more Love you send out, the more you will receive and the more you will have to give. The power of Love can heal the sick, feed the hungry, clothe the poor, shelter the homeless and put an end to poverty. It can save the environment, save endangered species and put an end to war!

Our social, economic and religious structures pit us against each other in so many ways. We need to realize that we are not contestants. We are not in competition with each other; this is illusion! The truth is that we are all related, and Love is the power that can bring us all together in peace and in harmony with each other and all of creation. This One Law truth can set us free.

The Law of One is all about inclusion, about the true equality of all humanity, irrespective of skin color, social class, landmass of origin or spiritual beliefs. *What dwells within the physical form is sacred and so must be honored.* What dwells within the human form is that which we must learn to honor in each other, and we must learn to allow each other to be free. The One Law is about freedom, the freedom to let the inner light within each of us shine through. It is about bringing forth into the physical world one's own unique expression of self, while allowing others to do the same. Why conformity? Control, control, control!

The One Law is also about the sanctity of Life, not only in the human sense, but Life in all its forms. To live and to let live. Inflicting pain, suffering or death upon any living thing goes against the One Law. Tiagorrah says:

*Life is the gift of Creator, and so must be honored in all things. Know that you are fortunate to have existence here on this, the most beautiful and abundant planet in the universe. Until recently there did exist a greater variety of Life forms here on planet Terra than upon any other world in the galaxy!*

The One Law is about the sacredness of the Earth. We need to understand that the Earth is a living thing and the source of all we need for our physical existence. We must cease attempting to reconfigure the natural environment. We must cease denuding the planet of its natural resources. We must cease driving untold numbers of other Life forms into extinction, while polluting the air, land and sea with our waste. We must change the way we regard the land, the seas, the air and all Life forms, for we are the *stewards of the Earth.*

The Law of One is also about the Creator's Love of infinite variety. Everything is unique, and everything, according to the Creator's intention, is interconnected to everything else within the cosmic scheme of things. I once saw a bumper sticker which read, Honor Diversity. Again, we must accept and honor this, because it is the intent of the Creator that these truths exist. These aspects of the One Law hold true whether you are a Hindu, Moslem, Christian or Jew. It doesn't matter what religion you practice, because we are all differing expressions, and these are merely differing avenues that lead to the same source. Truth is truth.

We need to simply allow each other freedom and learn to honor each other. The Law of One is simple, actually. It is about sharing and giving and honoring each other. Nobody should go without food, clothing, medicine or shelter. We do not need to spend millions and billions of dollars on weapons and war, and we don't need to destroy the planet to feed greed!

Knowledge and technology are neither good nor bad, positive nor negative. They just are. What you do with that knowledge and technology is the determining factor. Tiagorrah talks about the wondrous technology the ancient Atlanteans developed, but it didn't save them in the end, because they used it for negative and destructive purposes. He talks about their wonderful spiritual knowledge, but the One Law was distorted by the Temple of the Sun in order to bring about the Atlantean empire. You can use spiritual knowledge for positive or negative purposes. You can twist the truth to suit your own agenda.

I believe the Law of One is the ultimate truth that your heart and soul acknowledges deep within. By following and living the true principles of the Law of One, you will find what you have been searching for. You will attain peace and harmony within yourself and with the world around you. The truth shall set you free!

Before I close this piece, I want to include the following channeled information from Tiagorrah and another friend of mine, an entity identified as Standing Bear.

*It has been instilled in man to separate himself from those he perceives as differing from himself. It is taught that these strangers constitute a threat to security and well-being — this personally, institutionally, theologically and geographically as well. Through the ages there has been devised a spectrum of categories into which are deposited the vast multitude of humanity, division upon division, each according to distorted perceptions of appearance, behavior or thought.*

*Maps of the land are full of lines that separate it into pieces. These are nations, countries, all separate from each other. Sometimes they paint them different colors, saying, this is one land and this is another; this is one people and this is another. Now, look at one of the many pictures of the Earth taken from out there in space. Where are those lines that divide the lands? The only thing that divides the lands from each other are the waters. These lines are an illusion created by men!*

This is the message of these photographs: to free ourselves from that illusion and see ourselves and the Earth as One. We have reached a point in time and a level of technology that enables the Earth to speak to us through these pictures. I truly believe this. She shows us the ancient Mother — a fragile, blue-green orb adrift in space, alive and teeming with Life. I think she is showing us the circle, reminding us of the Law of One, and trying to stir our consciousness.

*Just as people have fought over and divided the lands, so have they divided themselves from each other. These display little acceptance and even less tolerance for others. It is fear and ignorance, controlled and manipulated by the negative elements, which leads to conflict.*

*Is the eagle more magnificent a creation than the wolf? No, each in its own way is equally magnificent, and the eagle and the wolf are brothers. Is the tiny flower less of a creation than the tall pine? Look to the great waters and to the sky. Which of these is the lesser or greater creation?*

*All people reflect miracles of the Creator's expression. The person standing before you is, in reality, merely the shell of one who, like the self, has worn many physical shells. There is coming a time when one will stand before another and celebrate both the uniqueness of each and the oneness of the two.*

*Share with each other the infinite diversity and variety of mankind! These differences in expression and culture are there not to divide people, but to enhance their experience and to broaden their conception of the All That Is. People must turn from their practices of division and instead embrace the concept of Oneness.*

*The Law of One is the ultimate truth which can set free all of humanity. It can raise the collective consciousness of mankind, thereby enabling same to break free from the cycles of his history, thus entering into a new age of enlightenment, Love and peace.*

# The Circle, the Fire and the Power of Ceremony

You are now on the continent of Atlantis, in the early times before the arrival of Poseidon. There is a fire ceremony this evening, and participants gather outside the east entrance of the ceremonial circle. The fire burns in the central fire pit and a priest now prepares the circle for ceremony. He first smudges himself with sage, then walks around the inside of the circle, smudging the whole area. It is now time for the participants to enter, but before doing so, the priest bathes each one in turn with the fragrant smoke. The purpose of smudging with sage is to cleanse and purify, to dissipate negative energies. Its use has many applications. Smudging clears out the auric field, drawing out impurities and expanding this energy field to its full capacity.

The priest opens the circle for ceremony. He must acknowledge the seven directions and call in the spirits and powers of creation. He begins in the east, going in turn to the four points of the wheel. He blows his breath upon the sage, holds it out in offering and calls upon the spirits and powers, the energies and elements. He asks that they pay attention and hear the prayers. He invites them into the circle to observe and participate in the ceremony. He is opening the doorways of the circle which lead to the Spirit world. He calls upon the Creator above and the ancient Earth Mother below in the same manner. Lastly, he acknowledges the Spirit within and declares the circle open and activated for ceremony. At this point energies are moving around, Spirit forces are entering and power is beginning to build up within the circle.

Everyone now begins drumming, as it is time for attunement to take place. The drum is the heartbeat of Life and the oldest instrument known to man. Its deep, rich tones reverberate through the physical body, expanding the auric field and stimulating the chakras. As all the participants fall into rhythm, there is opportunity for improvisation and variation. They are melding their vibrational energies together, tuning in to the same frequency. They are functioning together as one! Spirit forces entering in at this time help amplify this energy level within the circle. While the participants attune vibration, the sound emanations are attracting still more of the spiritual forces. The drumming continues until energy levels within the circle are at full capacity and all are in unison. Then the priest holds up his hand and the drumming ceases. There is silence.

The fire is now ready to receive prayers. At this point in the ceremony the priest approaches the fire for his own personal communion with Spirit. Then each individual in turn approaches the fire. Each has as much time as he or she requires to kneel before the fire and commune with Spirit. They kneel in silence and inwardly speak to Creator, ancestors, Spirit guides and helpers, or they choose to speak aloud their prayers. What transpires between them and the Creator is truly sacred, and as they kneel before the fire there is no such thing as time. At that point they are plugged into a direct, personal line to the Spirit world. When each communication is concluded, an offering is placed into the fire. When everyone has had a turn, then the priest again approaches the fire and says a prayer on behalf of all. When he has concluded this prayer, he places the final offering into the fire.

I would like to share with the reader the closing prayer that Tiagorrah taught me, one which I use at the end of the fire ceremonies I facilitate.

## Closing Prayer

Creator, Lifegiver, hear us! Hear the prayers we are making now. We give thanks for All That Is, and we thank you for our lives, our existence in the here and now. We make prayers now for all the people gathered here in this circle, that they might live long and find the things they seek in Life. Help them to have good health, great happiness and joy. Help them to realize Love and understanding. Help them to realize their Life purpose and guide them along a good pathway. This we ask of you now.

We make prayers now for all the people in the world who feel sorrow and pain, those who feel alone, forgotten or lost. For all the people who are hungry or without shelter. For all those who suffer from the effects of disease, war and poverty, we ask you to give them comfort and relief, give them nourishment and hope. This we ask of you now.

We make prayers now for all of our relations with whom we share the gift of Life — the four-leggeds, the winged people, the people of the waters, the green people and all creatures great and small upon the Earth. We ask that you look down on these beings and protect them from the excesses of mankind.

This we ask of you now.
We make prayers now for our Mother Earth,
she who freely gives to us all that we need to
live, she who is alive and abundant with
Life and all its splendid wonders! We
acknowledge this and give thanks for her
generosity. We ask that she be protected
from those who would do her harm.
We make these prayers now, together as one,
within this circle. And so it is!

The circle represents the many facets of Life in that it is a symbol of the continual cycles of Life. It represents the Life cycles that are constantly going on around us in the physical world. These are the cycles of spring, summer, fall and winter, the cycles of day and night, cycles of the moon, stars and planets. These are the cycles of birth, death and rebirth, reincarnation, the cycles of the soul's evolution. The circle also represents the law of karma, the law of cause and effect, of action and reaction. Whatever we say and do, whatever we send out into the world, will eventually return to us. It is a symbol of infinity, the continual evolution of all of creation. The ending of something is always the beginning of something new. These are the wheels within wheels, the cycles of existence set into motion by the Creative Force.

The circle represents the Law of One and is a sacred symbol throughout the universe in that it represents the Creator and all of creation. As everything within the circle is a part of the circle, so all of creation is a part of the Creator. Everything is interconnected within the cosmic scheme of creation. It is for this reason that spiritual ceremony has been carried out within the ceremonial circles since man's earliest beginnings. Tiagorrah comments on the importance of the circle by saying:

*The circle is that which signifies the Law of One, the universal law of inclusion and interconnection, the law of unity, harmony and balance, the law of Love. It is that which signifies the sacredness of the Earth as well as the cyclic nature of creation and the Spirit world.*

The fire at the center of the ceremonial circle can be seen to represent Life, the Life force or the soul. The dance of fire represents the dance of Life and the Life force that burns within us. It also represents the self, the individual, the physical being . . .

*The ceremonial fire could be seen as that which represents the focal point of the soul as projected forth into physical reality. This projection, which exists incarnate, perceives itself at the center of physical reality. Reality, then, is perceived from this singular vantage point.*

Because we perceive outward from center, we

acknowledge the seven directions. We are the fire at the center of the ceremonial circle. The fire is a beacon that draws in the spiritual elements and powers. It draws us together and we become one within the circle. The dance of fire is powerful, drawing inward and inducing a meditative state, an altered consciousness. It puts us in communication with Spirit and acts to amplify and transmit our energies.

The fire is the transmuter of energy. Whatever we put into the fire is changed, purified and sent off to the Spirit world. Thoughts are energy, and when we project our thoughts into the fire, that energy is transformed and radiated out to the realm of the nonphysical. We can put our doubts and fears into the fire, our illness, pain or anger. *In this way we can find release from those things which impede our spiritual growth and development.* I've seen people put letters, photos and packs of cigarettes into the fire. Some write on a piece of paper what they need to release, then place this into the fire.

Just as we can release, we can also receive energies from the fire. We can receive strength and courage, knowledge and understanding, help and healing. It is a gift to us, that we can utilize the fire in this way.

The fire ceremony is a powerful means of touching people and helping to raise their spiritual awareness. Tiagorrah says that other than reaching people through this book, the fire ceremony is the most important thing I am doing at this time. Other than the written word, the best way for me to really touch people with Tiagorrah's message is through the fire ceremony.

*The printed knowledge will be a powerful tool for spreading One Law consciousness, but I would that people also realize the power of ceremony to stimulate spiritual awakening and progression.*

Ceremony is a thing of Spirit when done from the heart. There is no right or wrong way to performing ritual, there are only *different* ways. Some say you have to do it this way and others that way, but the only thing that is important is that you approach it in the right manner and that you grow closer to Spirit.

The way I facilitate the fire ceremony is drawn from Tiagorrah's guidance, as many aspects of this ceremony are pure Atlantean ritual. Tiagorrah informs me that whether performed outside in a natural circle or inside the Temple of One Law in Poseidon, the basics of the ceremony are the same. Ritual within the ceremonial circle has continued through the many thousands of years, right up to the present day. Native Americans and other tribal peoples are responsible for having kept these ceremonial basics alive through heritage. There are many similarities between ancient Atlantean and modern tribal ceremonial practices.

*For those with the eyes to see, Atlantis' great influence over the Earth and her peoples remains visible in the world this day.*

There are two kinds of ritual ceremony, personal and public. A personal ritual is a powerful connection to Spirit; however, a ceremonial gathering, when attuned and amplified, can be more powerful. When a ceremonial site is used often, it becomes a powerful energy vortex.

When those who feel compelled to create either a personal or a ceremonial circle have found what they believe is a suitable site, they need to spend some time there in prayer and meditation. They need to make offerings of sage or incense until the Spirits and the Life forces of place gather around. As the ancient Atlantean Earth Keepers did ages ago, one must ask permission to utilize a site.

*You must listen and feel with your heart. Connect with place, consider all aspects and then the answer will come to you. With the blessing of the spiritual elements, the circle will truly be a sacred and protected place.*

The site of the circle is cleared and prepared by hand, without the use of tools. You have to get down on your hands and knees and humble yourself to the Earth as you construct the circle. The size depends on how many people are expected to participate in the ceremonies. It can be from a small personal space for an individual, up to a large ceremonial space, where any and all are welcome to attend.

The circumference of the circle can be marked with materials such as stones, mud bricks, hay bales and the like. Whatever is used to mark the circle is much less important than the power that will be inside it. There are special markers at the south, west and north points, and in the east is the open doorway. In the center of the circle is the fire pit. Stones or bricks are placed around the rim of this fire pit, and personal sacred objects such as stones, totems or jewelry can be placed upon them. It is like an altar, in that things placed here are cleansed and purified, touched by Spirit and charged with power.

The power of ceremony brings people together with Spirit. The circle brings both a connection to the physical reality of the Earth plane and a connection to the Spirit world.

*When you do this and make prayers in this way, then know that your prayers will be heard. If the Law of One touches your hearts, then walk with it, carry it with you. When others sense this in you and question, then share with them the knowledge.*

Here in Sedona I perform a fire ceremony weekly, and a full moon fire ceremony every month. In the ceremonial circle I see people from all walks of Life, from all across America and most other parts the world. Many of them tell me of being drawn to this land, being guided to the circle and the ceremony. During the ceremony we all become one, all of the same vibration together. The Law of One touches people and they open up to it. There is a familiarity to it because the ceremony awakens soul memory. The results are sometimes amazing. By end of the ceremony people are happy, renewed and empowered. Many of them tell me, "I've been looking for this for a long time." Perhaps we all have.

*Know that there are persons in the world for whom this information may spark soul remembrance of incarnations experienced ages ago in service of the One Law. There are many souls of Atlantean sojourn incarnate in the present reality. There will be those who understand and acknowledge this in themselves. There will be those who will be drawn to this knowledge and will embrace same. They will realize the importance of the reintroduction of One Law consciousness into the world at this time.*

*These awakened souls will go forth and walk with the knowledge, and it will go out from there. Thus the Word finds reintroduction and acknowledgment. Know that as more ceremonial circles appear in the world, so shall One Law consciousness increase.*

The ceremonial circle is an energy vortex in itself; the more ritual enacted within it, the more powerful that energy field becomes. In the circle there is awakening, enlightenment and transformation taking place; there is also healing, release and empowerment. Within the circle there is communication with the Spirit world, and past-life remembrances are accessible. I have seen this taking place within the ceremonial circle here in Sedona. Within that circle the One Law seed is planted, a spark is kindled and the spiritual journey begins or is wonderfully enhanced. I tell people to take the experience, the knowledge and the ceremony home with them. I tell them to utilize it, to incorporate it into their lives.

I can tell you from my own experience that there are ceremonial circles appearing all over America, all over the world! More and more people are creating ceremonial circles, and more and more people are coming together and making prayers in this way. In ever-increasing numbers, people are awakening to ancient, One Law knowledge and universal truth all over the Earth. Some feel compelled to create large ceremonial circles so that they can invite others to join them in ceremony. Others feel compelled to create small personal circles for their private use. Even if you simply arrange some crystals on your living room floor and light a candle in the center, the circle is your direct link to Creator and the All That Is.

# Opening to Channel

*Greetings. I would address a subject other than Atlantis at this time. I would speak as concerns Spirit world communication, as concerns opening the channel, so to speak. The physical vehicle is surrounded by the invisible world of Spirit. All is connected, thus those of you who wish to communicate with the Spirit plane can begin to do so now. Differences of spiritual preference are irrelevant at this time.*

*One who can access information from the Spirit world is known this day as a medium or channel. This could be described as a form of interdimensional energy transference. It is often received through what could be termed* conscious insertion.

*This is when the communication is inserted directly into the consciousness of the receiver, as is most commonly experienced. Everyone receives information from the surrounding spiritual forces. It is not strange or unusual in any way; it is not something supernatural. In times of need, in times of necessity, it is a perfectly natural mode of interdimensional communication.*

*You will hear no voices coming to you from out of the ethereal mist. An actual communication could take the form of a mere passing thought. One must learn to tune in and recognize these occurrences. The experience of conscience or of intuition, that small voice within — these are forms of Spirit communication. Sometimes ideas and insights that seem to come from out of the blue are, in actuality, that which has been inserted into the consciousness of the receiver.*

*In order to develop the ability to be more receptive to such transmissions, to perceive with more clarity, this does require the consistent practice of meditation. This is the key to expanding the ability. You must go inward to the self and yet open up to all around you. This requires attunement, at-one-ment, being in harmony with the Law of One.*

*Choose a time each day when you will be alone, where there will be no distractions. You may light a candle or burn a fragrant incense. You may choose to hear musical sound conducive to calming relaxation. You may choose to have only silence.*

*Situate the body in a reclined position of comfort. I suggest the use of a small meditation stone. There are a variety of stones that are good for this purpose. They are the Herkimer diamond, azurite, lapis, sugilite and fluorite of blue or purple. Place the stone at the third-eye chakra.*

*Now you must focus all thought and concentration upon this focusing object. You must see the stone in your mind's eye, feel the stone as it rests upon the forehead. If you listen closely, you can hear the sound of its vibration. You will feel the third-eye chakra as it unfolds and opens up.*

*This meditation must be practiced consistently, for no less than ten minutes every day. Eventually you will become aware of a bright light which appears to alter color and shape, there in the vision of your closed eyes. Know this as a Spirit light, and that it signals progress in attunement.*

*When this light appears with consistency, it is time to alter the meditation procedure. Now, before going into the altered state, contemplate your situation or formulate a question in your mind. Then when you enter the meditation, be mindful of what comes into your awareness, what thoughts or images, feelings or emotions you experience.*

*The beyond, from which originates such commu-*

*nication, is connected through the superconscious mind. From there, such communication passes through the subconscious into the conscious mind. Communication can also enter in through the crown chakra, if open and attuned. The most common form of transmission from Spirit is as a flow of knowledge coming into the awareness from the deepest realms of mind.*

*Other forms of manifestation of Spirit communication are as automatic writing and verbal channeling. In the instance of automatic writing, the physical vehicle would seem to be engaged in the act of taking dictation from the Spirit source, in this way manifesting the information in the form of the printed word. As to verbal channeling, the Spirit world and the incarnate share physical being on an audible, vocal level, in the same way as a radio. A radio receives the signal and then transforms it into sound. A channel translates the flow of spiritual transmission.*

*I would speak as concerns another form of Spirit communication — that of seeing images or visions, receiving information in the form of pictures, scenes and dreams. This may be termed interdimensional projection. Spirit, through the projection of images, attempts communication in this way as well.*

*You must attain the ability to utilize the power of the sixth chakra, the third eye, for this seeing. While in deep meditation, against the backdrop of darkness, stillness, silence, look here to see. At first, the presence of Spirit would appear as bright, swirling colors. Eventually, Spirit would impart symbols and images in communication.*

*The mind's eye may come to gaze upon the countenance of Spirit guides and helpers in this manner of seeing. Spirit may communicate on an audible level. You will not hear through physical ears, but as emanates more from within than from without.*

*I would speak as to the sleep state. Therein you are more receptive to psychic dreams. The sleep state is most conducive to reception, for there is little resistance from the conscious mind, and guides and helpers may choose to influence or direct the dreams, the images, to impart information in this manner. Spirit may choose to appear with a message or some advice. Thus you may see and hear these things on this level. Much communication takes place in the sleep state, in dreams.*

*I would speak as concerns doubt, questioning, difficulty in acceptance of such communication. Do not say, "Show me this so that I might believe that." Do not expect Spirit to form from out of a mist before your eyes. Do not listen in waiting for voices to call out to you from the ethereal stillness. Do not look for a tapping on the shoulder or for your television to go on and off in the middle of the night. Do not press for such things in order to relieve the doubts you may experience.*

*Again I tell you that the rational mind will conflict with that from the deeper levels of consciousness. The conscious mind does only accept that which is perceived through the five physical senses. The five physical senses relate only to the three-dimensional plane of experience. Therefore, anything which emanates from beyond that plane of existence will be questioned. Thus the rational mind will tend to dismiss such communication as nonreality. There is much going on around the physical being of which that being itself is unaware. When things such as these do come to the surface, it is only natural to question. Acceptance comes with time and with knowledge.*

*There are those who commonly see and hear Spirit. That which makes the difference for these is the fact that they have learned to trust Spirit. One believes in the Christ, not because He did knock upon the door and introduce Himself. It would be possible to awaken one night and see your protector standing at the foot of your bed, but do not look for these things to take place until the conditions are right for same.*

*I do present this knowledge in order that the way be made less difficult in these matters for those who would pursue these abilities. I would that you have a better idea of that which you may encounter. The way to Spirit, to things spiritual, to the universe, to the All That Is, is through the consistent practice of meditation. There is nothing strange or supernatural about this; it is a part of your natural ability to be able to communicate in this way. It is not that mankind has lost these abilities, it is simply that mankind has forgotten how to use them.*

# Conclusion

To early Atlanteans, the fluorite octahedron represented the two opposing forces that make up all aspects of reality. As the yin and yang symbol depicts positive and negative, black and white, male and female, so did the fluorite octahedron represent the same, and more, to ancient Atlanteans. No matter which way the stone is held, there are always two pyramids joined together at their base. To the Atlanteans, the two pyramids, pointing in opposite directions, stood for the Temple of the One Law and the Temple of the Sun. Fluorite represented then, and still does today, the balance that must be maintained between these two forces.

The reintroduction of One Law consciousness is

the counterbalance to the forces of the present-day Sons of Belial. Recorded history is testimony of their presence and manipulations. Their true goal for the next millennium is to reestablish the empire of Atlantis. They envision an empire so vast as to be all-encompassing, of a truly global scale. Their ultimate goals are a one-world government, a global capitalist economy and global religious unification under Christianity.

What is happening now in the world around us is simply the same thing that has happened before. All the problems we are currently facing, as we begin to move into the new millennium, are the same problems that plagued Atlantis ages ago. This time, however, the human population of the Earth is larger than it has ever been before. A vast number of souls are gathering here at this major turning point in mankind's evolution. Great numbers of these are ancient souls that have experienced lifetimes in Atlantis and Mu. Our population and our technological civilization are expanding at an ever-increasing rate, due to what Tiagorrah calls the time-compression effect.

Many predict that the Earth is incapable of sustaining a fully global, industrialized civilization. High-density population areas produce negative energies conducive to mind and thought control. Too many people living and working together in a limited environment creates great stress, especially when those involved are competing with each other for the golden apple. They have been programmed to believe the illusion that they are consumer-contestants living "The Price is Right." The sad part is that they perceive and accept this as normal.

I and many others believe that there is a one-world-oriented secret government operating in disguise over and above the United Nations. It works invisibly behind the scenes, and its members are the Illuminati of ancient secret societies. These are the modern-day Sons of Belial, whose roots stretch back to the Temple of the Sun. The intentions of Poseidon, Belial and Amillius are alive and well today!

Edgar Cayce predicted that a hidden chamber would be discovered at the foot of the Sphinx that contains ancient Atlantean knowledge and records. Scientists using the latest technology have indeed located an underground chamber beneath the paw of the Sphinx, as well as several other chambers and passageways within the Great Pyramid and elsewhere at the Giza site. Mystery and intrigue surround these discoveries as excavation and examination are being held up by Egyptian authorities.

*Manipulations are now taking place that will guarantee control over excavations and subsequent discoveries by the present-day high priests of the*

*Sons of Belial.*

The Sons of Belial are intent on the addition of this ancient Atlantean knowledge to their library of secret knowledge, which they use to further their aspirations of global domination.

The fall of communism and the spread of democracy set the stage for the introduction of a "new world order" for the next millennium. Get ready for it, because it's coming right at you. It's taking shape right now, right behind your back. Here in America, most live under the illusion that our government works to promote our well-being. We live under the illusion that we are free. Our democratic form of government is totally manipulated and controlled by the secret government. Governments worldwide are being manipulated toward this new world order.

Every day there are news reports concerning the global economy, global corporations and the global community. Newspaper, television and radio are full of reports about the global marketplace, the World Bank, the European Union, the United Nations and U.N. peace-keeping forces. There is a growing global capitalist economy that now influences most countries, including Russia and China. The spread of this consumption-based system of economic enslavement is publicized as the spread of free enterprise. Like a wolf in sheep's clothing, those in control are not advocating or demonstrating

One Law consciousness. What they are attempting to put into place is a far cry from the Law of One.

It is more apparent with every passing day that all forms of the media are completely controlled and manipulated by the secret government. One need only observe thirty minutes of the Cable News Network to see the manipulation of news. More time is devoted to trivia and media hype. This is intended to divert the public's attention from factual, relevant news reporting. We are told only what we are permitted to know and shown only what we are permitted to see. The result is that we are programmed by the programs! Flashing imagery, disinformation, sound and vibrational conditioning—this is ancient Atlantean mind control!

Through the centuries of recorded history there have been movements among the organized religions to either convert others to their own belief system or to, quite literally, do away with them. This has not only aided the secret Illuminati in controlling the masses, but it has permitted them to outlaw and stamp out any trace of One Law belief or practice wherever it could be found. The modern-age Sons of Belial have played off one religion against another to further their agenda, just as they play countries against each other for the same purpose. Today there is a movement among various religious authorities toward unification, or absorption, into a one-world religion. Again, this is not One Law consciousness at work here.

There is a greater religion sweeping the world at this time. This one-world religion grows stronger and more powerful every day. It is a religion of wealth, power and greed that stands for unlimited growth, expansion and abundance. It promotes separation and exclusion, enslavement and thought control. This is the religion of the Temple of the Sun, of the Sons of Belial. They have been centralizing economic, political and religious power since the beginning of recorded history. They are good at it, because their experience dates back to a time before Atlantis' rise to power.

Man is constantly being controlled by the world around him. The media, the government and religion are constantly telling him how he must live his Life. Yet when he follows their directions, he wonders why he feels there is still something missing. He strives harder to achieve and to conform, yet becomes only more dissatisfied, frustrated and confused. He's following the program, but he cannot find the peace, happiness and satisfaction that was promised if he did so.

People are programmed to believe that everyone must conform, to think and act alike. Our society is set up to stifle individuality and promote mindless conformity. People are so programmed and conditioned that they police each other, for anyone who does not conform is considered strange, weird or just plain crazy. They imitate each other to the point where they lose their inner sense of identity. There is also a loss of the diversity, customs and distinctions that are a part of the rich abundance of existence. The world around us thus becomes more uniform and more impersonal.

The last thing the Sons of Belial want you to realize is the Law of One. They certainly don't want you to realize your own divinity and connection to the All That Is. The reason they can conduct themselves in this way and continue to progress their goals is because there is little counterbalance to check the progress of their negative influences. As long as this continues, the Sons of Belial have free reign to progress their agenda.

People must no longer allow themselves to be manipulated and controlled. They must wake up to what is happening and take back control of their minds and lives. We are all here for a purpose; there is something that each of us is here to learn and accomplish. If we conform to the system's demands, we stifle our own divine purpose for being. What everyone needs to realize is that we are all Spirits who have taken on human form. Tiagorrah refers to the physical body as the perfected vehicle. It is a Life-support system. The body is merely a vehicle the Spirit inhabits in order to fulfill a purpose on the Earth plane. If we believe that the body is who we are, then we live in illusion.

We need to free up our minds so that we can think. We need to boldly challenge beliefs that have been held sacrosanct throughout history. The Law of One flies in the face of present authority, because it rejects blind obedience to dogma and encourages the psychological and spiritual development of the individual. Human beings are, in essence, a microcosm of the greater universe. "Know thyself" was carved above the doorway of Apollo's temple at Delphi. Self-knowledge, going within the self, is the true path through which to reconnect with one's own divine origins. This is why it is important to reintroduce One Law consciousness at this time. It has all but been negated, repressed throughout history to the point where negative influences run rampant in the world.

*The Word, the information which does find emergence from out of the vortices of Sedona at this time, will be the final spiritual promptings before mankind's committal to a more difficult transition. By the time of the occurrences, the information and knowledge channeled through these doorways will have been expended forth. At the time of the events described, Sedona will have been developed to the point where the introduction of negative energy into the area will be saturate. This is a deliberate attempt by the Sons of Belial to negate that which is a positive and enlightening center of spiritual attraction and stimulation. The day shall arrive of cleansing. These will be the last rays of Light to issue forth from Sedona.*

The agents of profit and greed are certainly at work here in Sedona, but I feel the energies building up around here for a great spiritual campaign to burst forth. I know of others who have been summoned here by Light forces in order to take up the work of reintroducing the Law of One to those who are themselves being called to higher consciousness. There are many prophecies and speculations as to what will occur, and how devastating the Earth changes will be. It is extremely important for people to realize that what will take place depends on the levels of higher consciousness and positive energy in the world. It is vital for each individual to awaken to higher spiritual truths, to embrace the One Law, thereby helping to raise world consciousness and create a smoother transition into a new age of enlightenment.

Those who hold up the actions of our leaders to scrutiny, those who question what we as a collective stand for, these are the true patriots . . . patriots of humanity. At this crucial point in the history of the Earth and mankind, it is extremely important that those who are questioning and seeking the truth are given help and encouragement.

*As humanity enters into the new millennium, there must be increase in free thought and elevation of consciousness.*

The more truth that is introduced into people's lives and the more awareness they have of what is transpiring around them, the more they come to understanding. Then they will be empowered to seek ways to decrease their participation and dependency on the machine and increase their personal freedom. They will come together to create alternatives and take back control of their lives rather than continue to allow their lives and minds to be controlled.

Those who judge their self-worth by the opinions of others, by the amount and value of their material possessions, by their job title and social standing, are slaves to the system, living in illusion and contributing to the problem. People must simplify their lives, become more self-sufficient and learn to live in harmony with each other, the Earth and all other Life forms.

We are at a major turning point in the evolutionary processes of the Earth and mankind. Changes must be brought into effect, for we cannot continue in the present manner. There are many messengers trying to wake people up and bring them into awareness. The more people embrace higher spiritual truths and raise their consciousness, the easier the transition period will be for humanity as a whole. We each have an important part to play in what lies ahead.

People everywhere are being called upon to consciously reconnect with their higher selves, their link to the Source, and open wide the lines of communication with Spirit guides and helpers. These will assist us to distinguish reality from illusion and help us prepare for, and direct us through, this time of transition. If you have not done so already, begin the regular practice of meditation, such as described by Tiagorrah. Help and assistance is available from the Spirit world; we need only to open up the lines of communication.

*If we can change our minds, we can begin to change the world. If we can acknowledge the Earth as a living being, then we can begin to heal the planet. If we can understand that all is interconnected within the cosmic scheme of creation, then we can live in harmony. Such is the Law of One.*

— *Tiagorrah*

W. T. Samsel, author

# AFTERWORD

I have been a musician, songwriter and vocalist in New York, Denver and St. Louis: I have owned and operated several retail outlets for Native American art and was a northern traditional dancer at pow-wow gatherings in the Midwest. My interests are similarly diverse, ranging from nature to science fiction, from model airplanes to personal computers, from playing Native American flute to the mystical sounds of the sitar.

Creator loves infinite variety. That's the wonder of existence — to experience and to learn all we can. I've been a channel all my Life, and for a long time couldn't understand it. What is channeling anyway? It's when you are able to tap into a higher source. That is exactly what artists do. Channeling mostly creative energy, I came into progression and understanding when I met Ruth Seals, a gifted light-worker who became my teacher. Spiritual doors began opening up for me at that time.

I was guided to Sedona because the energies here are conducive to spiritual growth and development. Ruth had told me that I would be guided to work in a truly sacred land. I had read somewhere about Sedona, but never imagined myself living here and doing the work in which I am presently engaged. Spirit guided me here in order to begin doing this work.

One of the things I do is perform deep, soul-level Crystal and Tarot card readings for people. We get into why you are the person you are, why your individual circumstances may be as they are and, most important, what you need to do to change things and progress spiritually. I find most people are guided to this reading. I am directed to give them prescriptions for certain crystals and healing stones and directions on how to utilize them. I may be directed to give them certain meditations to practice. With the right tools, it is easy for people to experience progression, to effect positive change in their lives. They can communicate with Spirit guides and helpers and become aware of and use the gifts and abilities they have brought into the incarnation.

Ten years ago, when my own perception was opening up, was a very wonderful and exciting time for me. I can still recall the essence of that period. I want it to be so for those who are guided to me for this service. Everything I do is to promote the Law of One, the universal law of interconnection and inclusion. This is the purpose of my work as a spiritual practitioner and ceremonial facilitator.

All of my ritual and ceremonial work is carried out within the circle. The ceremonial circle, with the fire at its center, predates recorded history by tens of thousands of years. The ritual work I do within the circle is drawn from Spirit, guided by Spirit and is for the most part Atlantean. The circle is the symbol of the Law of One. It all goes back to the original religion of an ancient people you won't find in the history books. I presently conduct Full Moon and Fire ceremonies here in Sedona. These are open to everyone, and all are welcome to attend. I also perform various personal ceremonies.

Now that *The Atlantis Connection* has been completed, the work of promotion is under way. It is extremely important that this information be disseminated to as many people as possible at this critical time in the history of mankind and the Earth.

— W. T. Samsel

You can write to the author at:

The Atlantis Connection
135 Pony Soldier Rd.
Sedona, AZ 86336

To secure Mr. Samsel for an interview or book-signing event or to sponsor a speaking engagement, contact Lorna Smith at (520) 203-0703.

---